MOFFIES

Gay Life in Southern Africa

by Bart Luirink

An imprint of David Philip Publishers, Cape Town

First published in English in Southern Africa by Ink Inc., an imprint of David Philip Publishers, 208 Werdmuller Centre, Newry Street, Claremont 7708, South Africa

© 1998, 2000 Bart Luirink, Johannesburg

Originally published in Dutch by Uitgeverij Jan Mets, Amsterdam, The Netherlands, in 1998, under the title *Moffies: Homo- en lesboleven in het zuiden van Afrika*.
Published in translation by arrangement with Uitgeverij Jan Mets, Amsterdam

ISBN 0-86486-442-6

Translation © 2000 Loes Nas
Copyedited by Giles Griffin

All rights reserved

Cover artwork: 'Untitled' by Alwyn Petersen, enamel on plywood, 1999. Collection Karen Rolfes
Cover design: Viva la Vida

Printed by Rustica Press, Old Mill Road, Ndabeni, Cape Town
D7934

This translation is sponsored by a financial contribution from Hivos, the Dutch Humanistic Institute for Development Cooperation.
For more information contact:
Hivos, Raamweg 16, 2596 HL The Hague, The Netherlands
Tel.: 070 376 55 00 Fax: 070 362 46 00
E-mail: hivos@hivos.nl Website: www.hivos.nl

Preface

It was February 1998, shortly before I left my job in Johannesburg to travel to Zimbabwe, when a fellow journalist anxiously enquired whether I would be safe. President Mugabe's speech made in mid-1995 – which included the infamous line 'gays are perverts and their behaviour is worse than that of pigs' – effectively declared open season on homosexuals. Gays suddenly seemed to have become a somewhat endangered species. Fortunately the situation was not as bad as it sounded. In Harare I found the headquarters of the gay movement in a luxurious, overcrowded mansion.

In Namibia a similar attack by President Nujoma had led to the establishment of a gay movement. In Botswana and Swaziland there were at least initiatives to get gay organisations off the ground. So in these countries, it was not too difficult to find guides to introduce me to the gay scene.

As a matter of course it was easy for me, as a gay person, to meet other gays. And many of them wanted to talk – loudly and without having to worry about who was listening. In this way I heard a number of both sad and cheerful stories. These are the stories on which this book is based.

Everywhere the condemnation of homosexuality as

'Western', and therefore 'un-African', by Mugabe and his allies was rejected – and that rejection was frequently supported by the evidence of both personal experience and published literature. Marc Epprecht, lecturer in the Department of History at the University of Zimbabwe, refers to the rock art of the San people which offers 'the first evidence of (group) sex between men at least over a thousand years ago'. In his essay titled 'Homosexual "Crime" in Early Colonial Zimbabwe (1892–1923)' Epprecht offers yet more indisputable evidence. He writes: 'In 1921 a Mazoe chief told the magistrate of Bindura that native law prescribed a penalty of one piece of cattle in the case of sodomy. Which suggests in itself that sodomy was not considered to be a serious crime. Incest commanded six cattle, adultery eleven.' In another legal document from 1915, an Achewa speaks the following words: 'I do not deny the accusation. In my country, Malawi, it is customary to commit sodomy if one cannot get a wife.'

Oliver Phillips, an academic from the Institute for Criminology at the University of Cambridge, studied Zimbabwean law and came to the conclusion that 'like in other parts of Africa, there are indications that the attitude towards same-sex sexuality varied between the different tribes: some ignored it, some institutionalised it in rituals, and some punished it'. Like Epprecht, he comes to the conclusion that there is a 'culture of silence' in Africa, which may well be the result of a vacuum created under the influence of urbanisation.

As a result of this movement into urban areas, old customs were abandoned. Likewise the traditional inclusion of sex education in initiation rituals fell away. Modern schools, usually established by missionaries, replaced this education – and often erased it altogether. They virtually declared sex to be taboo. Following this reasoning, it is indeed fair to say that Western influence did give homosexuality a bad name in Africa.

Homophobic legislation in a number of southern African countries confirms this shift, as it usually goes back to the colonial era and is based on a staunchly conservative Victorian morality. For that reason there are no provisos in African legislation (except later in South Africa) for a lesbian way of life. Queen Victoria herself simply could not imagine such things to exist.

Another indication that Phillips' and Epprecht's analyses are accurate lies in the story of the proposed legislative changes which the South African National Party presented to the white minority Parliament in 1968. Until then, homosexuals could be prosecuted only if they were caught in the act. You were actually allowed to be a homosexual but woe betide you if you were a *practising homosexual* (let alone an expert). The argument was that homosexuality 'was a threat to Western civilisation'. The proposed legislation was shelved after a (white) homosexual lobby made a significant fuss.

There is something strange about the desire to prove that homosexual behaviour is not necessarily white and definitely black. During a session at the annual conference of the International Gay and Lesbian Association in September 1999 one mlungu after another cited examples of homosexuality within an endless number of tribes. One of the participants wondered whether 'this was not a reactionary attitude?' Mugabe, and subsequently the Presidents of Namibia, Zambia, Kenya and Uganda, have characterised homosexuality as un-African, after which a parade of anthrohomo-apologists have anxiously tried to find evidence of the opposite.

I have often been reminded by the people I have spoken to that homosexual behaviour manifests itself more often than many imagine in the silent, African twilight zone: in the remote cattle post, where herdsmen enjoy each other's company; in the single-sex hostels, where until recently mineworkers regularly 'entered into matrimony'; and in prisons. In his work

Apostles of Civilised Vice: Immoral Practices and Unnatural Vice in South African Prisons and Compounds, South African activist Zackie Achmat disputes the notion that these practices should be viewed solely as a 'substitute' for lack of women. 'Special circumstances offer conditions for liberation, for discovering a new sexuality. [...] It is simply impossible that these "marriages" and other less formal expressions of sexuality would occur if the persons concerned would not regard the male torso as a bodily garden of delight in the first place.'

In addition, it is wrong to think that Mugabe and Nujoma were the first to make an issue of homosexuality in southern Africa. It was the gay and lesbian movement of South Africa that convinced the ANC leadership, during the CODESA negotiations before the democratic elections in 1994, that the struggle for freedom and the struggle for gay rights were inseparable.

The consequence was a constitution that is almost unanimously praised around the world – and it specifically outlaws discrimination on a variety of grounds including 'sexual orientation'. This is internationally unparalleled, and it encouraged the gay movement in Zimbabwe to register for the annual book fair in Harare in order to distribute folders and brochures that would call a (gay) spade a spade.

Because that is what it boils down to: until then in southern Africa homosexuality was quite literally unmentionable. It has always been part of the past, it is part of the present and everybody knows about it – they just don't talk about it.

Mugabe is right in one sense when he accuses Westerners of thrusting a phenomenon onto Africa. It is not homosexuality as such that has been imported, but rather a set of far more open and visible expressions of it – a supposed liberation that has developed over some time in the West. The possibility of going public, of identifying with others, means people no longer feel isolated. And can southern African homosexuals be blamed for wanting to exchange the lonely secrecy of the closet for the solidarity and camaraderie gained from an openly avowed gay identity?

Bart Luirink
Johannesburg

Acknowledgements

With thanks to Jack Lewis, Zackie Achmat, Tina Machida, Keith Goddard, Nyasha Mpungo, Patrick, Mike, Joe, Lester, Nini van Driel, Daan van Alten, Marijke Overeem, John van't Hoff, Simon Nkoli, Graeme Reed (Gay and Lesbian Archives/Johannesburg), Ian Swartz, Steven Scholtz, Liz Frank, Alice Mogwe, *Sister Namibia*, Robert Teunissen, Azim Koning, Michael, Kefuoe, Anita Dries, Maria Kint.

When writing this book I found useful background information in *Defiant Desire* (Johannesburg, 1994), a collection put together by Mark Gevisser and Edwin Cameron on homosexuality in South Africa, and in *The Island* (Cape Town, 1996), a collection on Robben Island edited by Harriet Deacon.

Some passages were published in a different form in the weekly magazine *Nieuwe Revu* (The Netherlands), the daily newspapers that are part of the *Zuid-Oost Pers* (The Netherlands), the *Mail and Guardian* (South Africa) and the magazine *Zuidelijk Afrika* (The Netherlands).

At the request of some of the people referred to, their names have been changed.

'Tonight I need a really good fuck,' says Elias. He does not make any secret of his innermost feelings. He looks about twenty years of age, definitely no older. He has short dreadlocks and wears Malcolm X glasses. As if to underline his need he continues: 'Can I book you?'

Smiling, his one hand resting perkily on his left hip, the other playing with a bunch of keys, he patiently awaits my answer. Lots of thoughts cross my mind:

He hardly knows me. What does he see in me? What risks will I be taking? I do not have any condoms on me. He is very beautiful though. Would he want to be paid? I don't know my way around: how do I get back to my hotel?

Slightly offended by such substantial and visible hesitation, Elias decisively interprets my unspoken considerations: 'Your loss,' he says in a resigned manner, 'but friends nevertheless.' And he walks off.

This is my first night in South Africa. It is October 1990, about six months after Nelson Mandela's release and the legalisation of the African National Congress (ANC). The country is torn between hope and fear. There are indications of change but the official negotiations on the transition to democracy have not yet begun. The liberation of the remaining political prisoners and the return of tens of thousands of exiles are endlessly frustrated by the old guard still in power. They make a firm decision to keep hold of the reins in the transformation process. The conflict between the ANC and the Inkatha movement, fuelled by the South African police, spills over from Natal into other parts of the country. The newspapers carry daily reports of new victims, new bloodbaths.

That first day feels like a warm bed in which I have made a particularly soft landing. Shortly after my arrival, I follow the advice given to me over the phone by my South African friends, whom I met when I was working for the anti-apartheid movement in The Netherlands.

'You're staying in Yeoville? Then you must go to Crackers. That's where you'll find everybody!' And indeed, in this coffee shop in Rockey Street I meet several old friends, whom I knew from time spent together in Amsterdam and London.

'You're arriving on Friday?' Simon Nkoli had asked. Simon was chairperson of GLOW (Gays and Lesbians of the Witwatersrand), the multi-racial organisation in Johannesburg, whom I had got to know a year before during his whistle-stop visit to Amsterdam. After participation in an ILGA conference (International Lesbian and Gay Association) in Sweden, he was happy to take up an invitation from people involved in COC, the Dutch gay and lesbian movement, to make a stopover in The Netherlands on his return.

'Why don't you come to the Skyline in the evening?' Simon continued. 'It's always very crowded. You go to Hillbrow, Pretoria Street. On your left, upstairs at the Shoe Repairs sign, next to the Harrison Reef Hotel.'

❦❦❦

'Welcome to Mandela's,' smiles the bartender, shaking my hand. Gay South Africa has apparently got high expectations of the recently liberated ANC leader. I have just climbed the red-carpeted stairs to the establishment, leaving Hillbrow behind with its neon adverts, street children and howling sirens, and on to the passionate sounds emanating from the jukebox and the screeches of the Skyline clientele.

You feel so much more freedom of movement when you're abroad. In Amsterdam it took me years to pluck up the courage to go into gay bars on my own, where I sat myself down in a dark corner and waited for hours until somebody cared to look in my direction. Which only happened occasionally, and even then I always left the bar alone. Even in a packed dark room, I managed to stay untouched – if only to find out in better light that men who were even older and uglier than me had managed to find satisfaction. So up until that first evening in South Africa, I was convinced that I would be leading an almost sexless life forever. To be honest, my self-esteem was in a very bad way.

But Mandela's, also known as Skyline, put a solid dent into this fatalistic outlook on life on that first evening, for it was not only Elias who made a proposition. Thabo did so too. Immediately after we got acquainted, he pulled out his diary and asked when and where would suit me. And then there was Jabulani, who did not beat around the bush at all and just said: 'Come on, let's go.' It took a concerted effort to go home alone that evening. The advances were so overwhelming that I was completely bowled over. Totally confused, I forgot to ask myself why it was that I wanted to go 'home' on my own anyway.

Skyline differs in more than one respect from all those well-established and self-consciously smart gay bars in Amsterdam. There is, for instance, a complete lack of interior design. It is a more or less barren space twenty-five metres long and fifteen metres wide. It has a concrete floor. There are bright red roller blinds that block the view onto a passage to which you can retreat to chat on plastic garden furniture. There are benches along the walls and more than a third of the space is taken up by a basic but very friendly bar. Behind that bar you'll find two black middle-aged men. Happy family men from Soweto, I was told that first evening. Their names are Norman and Stephen, so you can regularly hear young guys shrieking for the attention of 'Norma!' or 'Stephanie!'

Moving on, there is a billiard table and a jukebox which plays 'One Night in Heaven' at regular intervals throughout the evening. Whenever this happens, the crowd suddenly starts moving together and you could be forgiven for thinking you're watching the filming of a Michael Jackson music video.

The patrons themselves, and the odd poster with a half-naked male torso, indicate that this is not a 'run-of-the-mill' pub. Indeed, it is the patrons that provide the colour at Skyline, and they are so attractive that any attempt to distract your attention with its interior design would be doomed to fail.

Speaking of colour, the number of whites in the bar can be counted on the fingers of one hand. And then there's another unusual phenomenon: every hour or so a toupéed man in his fifties pops up out of the blue – a pigeon-chested white guy with a touched-up Hitler moustache. First he stares around the room and then he takes a trip around it in almost military style, waving a small knobkerrie, which he holds in his left hand, as he goes. When everything seems to be in order, he disappears again. This is, according to Norman, the proprietor of the hotel next door, whose survival is almost entirely due to the trade done in this bar.

Over and above the propositions, the conversation is often influenced by the turbulent political developments in the country. Skyline is the meeting place for political activists, students, street kids and sex workers. The South African rent-boy equivalent likewise demonstrates a strong distaste for beating around the bush.

And you will not meet any women here. They are not allowed in, whether they are lesbian or not. Of course, there is a priest floating around, who never tires of saying that he approves. Jozef, one of his disciples, tries to convince me to visit the gay church the next Sunday, which meets in an upstairs room at the hotel next door. Meanwhile, he slips a pack of condoms into my hand. His church has organised a condom drop for that night. 'They are free,' says Jozef. 'They have been made available by the municipality of Johannesburg.' He adds: 'Make the most of it …'

It is almost closing time when Simon Nkoli switches off the jukebox and urges the remaining customers to join South Africa's first 'Pink Saturday' the following day.

Three propositions and eight rounds of drinks later, I leave the pub and go home, a little unsteadily. 'Are you sure?' asks Elias, whom I come across a few hundred metres later. In my pocket I feel the condoms scratch invitingly against my palm.

▾▾▾

It seems like the devil's work … the day after my arrival in South Africa GLOW has organised its first-ever public parade. It is an overcast Saturday morning and in one of the rooms at the South African Institute of Race Relations a few hundred of the very bravest gay activists have come together. Solidarity telegrams from around the world are read aloud. There are speakers: an Afrikaans dominee (minister) who has just deserted the Dutch Reformed Church; a militant dyke by the name of Bev; and Simon Nkoli, chairperson of GLOW. 'I'm fighting for the abolition of apartheid,' he says. 'And I fight for the right of freedom of sexual orientation. These are inextricably linked with each other. I cannot be free as a black man if I am not free as a gay man.' His speech meets with thundering applause, after which the marchers gather and move off.

We walk in the rain through a desolate Braamfontein – on a Saturday morning this business district is entirely deserted – and into Hillbrow, passing by Johannesburg's municipal offices.

Black domestic workers cheer on the demonstrators from the surrounding balconies and roofs.

Many men and women in the parade have put brown paper bags over their heads for fear of being recognised. At the head of the parade, the drag queens are out in full force, drawing a lot of attention. Like drag queens everywhere else in the world, they are ashamed of nothing and regularly make the many onlookers laugh. It is actually only the odd fellow demonstrator who is annoyed by the ladies. 'It's them you'll see on the front page of the newspaper tomorrow,' says John, who shows no sign of being gay. Come to think of it, he shows no sign of being interesting in any way.

Every hundred metres or so, the demonstrators are addressed by a religious fundamentalist from the kerb. He confidently predicts the participants' progress towards hell and damnation. 'We have been in tighter spots,' Simon says level-headedly.

In Pieter Roos Park, where the number of interested people keeps growing, there are more speeches and performances by, among others, a group of gumboot dancers from Soweto: young guys with sweaty torsos, who give an excellent performance of the traditional mineworkers' dance, regularly slapping their rubber boots. Whether they are gay or not, nobody knows, but they are there ... so what does it matter? At the end of the afternoon, Nkoli exhorts those present to embrace their left neighbour and give him or her a big fat kiss on the mouth. This is a provocation of the highest order in a country where until recently hardly anything was permitted in public – let alone a homosexual kiss.

Some white participants stand momentarily in shock, realising all of a sudden that they are standing next to a black person. And they quickly brace themselves to do as Nkoli urges, leaving history behind.

I am standing next to John.

▼▼▼

You can clearly see Simon Nkoli's disappointment in his face when he opens one of two boxes sent to him from Hong Kong. A friendly organisation has sent a couple of thousand of condoms, but when he takes one out of its foil and rolls it out, its circumference appears to be very modest. 'This won't be much use here,' he quips.

The boxes take up considerable space in Nkoli's equally modest cottage. For a few months now he has been living in the old domestic servant's quarters behind a lawyer friend's house.

It's a few days after that first Pink Saturday and the telephone rings constantly. '*Bona*, a black monthly, printed my telephone number in the interview. Now I get phone calls from all sorts of people who want information about GLOW. That is great, but in the process I'm told a lot of sad stories. This sometimes makes me a bit depressed,' Nkoli says, after he has promised for the umpteenth time to send somebody a registration form. After our coffee, he quickly gathers some documents together and picks up two dildoes, putting them both in a plastic bag. It is suddenly clear to me why Chinese condoms would be useless in South Africa.

'When you come to South Africa again, you must let me know. Then you can bring a couple of new ones,' Nkoli says. 'You cannot get them here – they are prohibited – and we need them for our workshops on safe sex.'

While images of my next arrival in South Africa flash through my mind – a customs officer first staring at his screen for a long time, then having to consult his colleague – I promptly promise to comply with his request.

'I first have to deliver this bag to my office in Soweto – a colleague is taking a workshop for me this afternoon. She needs the dildoes. After that I will visit my mother in Sebokeng. Feel like coming along?' he asks, locking the door.

The minibus taxi takes about half an hour to reach its destination. We are squashed in with fourteen other passengers. The radio is at its loudest: only the strident horn, with which the driver constantly announces his presence, is able to drown out the music. Next to me a friendly old woman valiantly attempts to control a live chicken. We drive away from town, along the highway toward the township that is slowly coming into view before us.

'The train is much cheaper,' shouts Nkoli, 'but since armed gangs jump in and out of the trains, shooting wildly, we are too scared to travel that way.' These mysterious attackers, whenever they strike, sow growing doubts on the intentions to bring about a peaceful negotiated transition to democracy.

'The taxis are safer, even if they drive like maniacs,' Nkoli explains as the driver brings the vehicle to a brakes-squealing standstill in front of Baragwanath Hospital. Bara, as it is popularly known, is the largest hospital in Africa with over 3000 beds. It towers over the low-rise buildings so characteristic of Soweto. On our way to another taxi which will take us to White City Jabavu, I see a lot of houses – as far as the eye can see – all the size of the proverbial matchbox. The vegetable hawkers near the taxi ranks, the endless hooting, the smell of braaiwors, the smoke that hangs low over the township and the immense mass of people ... all of a sudden I have landed in the reflected shadow of a white world. A white face immediately stared at in a friendly way by passers-by. 'Welcome to Soweto, bru,' shouts one of the drivers. 'Feel at home among us dangerous darkies.'

Simon takes me by the hand and pushes me into another taxi.

The office of the Township AIDS Project (TAP), where Nkoli works as a sex education officer, is part of the Anglican Ipelegeng Centre. It is a ramshackle Wendy house behind the church, full of posters encouraging safe sex. It had opened for business only a few months before, launched by funding from Scandinavian development organisations.

'We don't get any financial support from the government. They have said for a long time that the disease doesn't exist here and now De Klerk thinks it is only a black problem,' Nkoli says bitterly.

It is true that the virus took its time to reach South Africa – possibly one of the few positive consequences of the isolation of the country for all those years – but it has since hit home mercilessly and Nkoli's colleagues in the organisation are convinced that the majority of the patients in Bara are suffering from it. 'But people pull the wool over each other's eyes and say that their next-of-kin died of TB. The newspapers do nothing to discourage this misunderstanding.'

The Township AIDS Project wages a lonely battle against denial in a world in which any discussion about sexuality is taboo. In the waiting room of the office, the organisation's volunteers outbid each other with an endless stream of stories testifying to a heady mix of prejudice, ignorance and ridicule.

'Men,' said Themba, 'are totally unaware. They fuck around until they drop and if they fall ill, they blame their wives.'

'Some sangomas allege that you can get rid of the virus by having sex with a baby,' Dorothy reported.

'Sex is only lekker if it is flesh to flesh,' Nkosinathi heard last week from a participant in one of the workshops.

'And AIDS means American Invention to Discourage Sex,' a workshop participant explained matter-of-factly.

'I don't wear a raincoat in the shower, do I?' somebody else objected when Nkoli demonstrated how to roll on a condom with the aid of a dildo.

It is a 'Western' disease. It is an invention of apartheid designed to decimate the black population. It only affects gays. The TAP workers have heard all these stories many times before.

'In Africa AIDS affects heterosexuals first,' says Nkoli. 'According to doctors in Bara, at least twenty thousand pregnant women in Soweto have been infected by the virus. But again, as elsewhere, it is gay people that took the lead in the fight against AIDS.'

Everybody agrees.

'It is truly tragic that, as the country finally gets rid of apartheid, many of its people will not be able to enjoy that new-found freedom for long. In the struggle against oppression, South Africa at least had means at its disposal – defiance campaigns, strikes, armed attacks, boycotts, international solidarity – which could put practical pressure on the situation. But in the fight against AIDS we are powerless. Everyone is waiting for the vaccine ... and if they ever create one, Africa will probably not be able to afford it.'

In the autumn of 1990 Nkoli is one of the very few who seem to be aware of this tragedy. This is perhaps partly because his commitment to the fight against apartheid is closely linked to his struggle against AIDS – and for gay rights.

'I'm a born activist,' he says on the road from Soweto to Sebokeng, a black township south of Johannesburg, not far from Sharpeville. His beard and leathers make him appear larger than he really is. Armed with a lethal combination of eloquence and wit, it is easy for him to attract and keep people's attention. While travelling on public transport, he tends to bring up the sensitive subject of his sexual preference. He shows no shame in doing so and sees no need to make excuses. With him, what you see is what you get. On the way to Sebokeng, some passengers listen to him in silence as he tells them he is a 'moffie'. Others nod in approval. Deftly employing his disarming sense of humour, he soon has them laughing.

'Mandela lies in bed on the evening after his release and Winnie enters the bedroom. The old man is already half asleep when she starts making advances. Softly she strokes his hair and then puts her hand under the blankets. Whereupon Mandela wakes up and mumbles: "Not tonight, Sisulu."'

The idea of a prison romance between the ANC leader and Walter Sisulu, his fellow freedom fighter on Robben Island, makes everyone roar with laughter. Furthermore, any allusion to Winnie's alleged sexual activities is always guaranteed to raise a smile with South Africans.

'Not tonight, Sisulu.' The passengers in the taxi keep on repeating the phrase.

'This closet could tell quite a story,' says Nkoli when we arrive at his mother's tiny house. This, Zone 14 in Sebokeng, is where he grew up. Leaning against the closet, he says: 'We lived here illegally. We are Sotho and under apartheid only Xhosas were allowed to live here. The system not only kept white and black separate, but the right to live in a specific township was also tribally determined.' His mother moves with difficulty to the sink in the small room, which is crammed with far too much furniture. Nkoli is irritated by the chink of the crockery she takes out of the closet: in this house his natural authority clearly carries less weight.

'Why don't you sit down?' he says in an agitated voice, but Elizabeth has heard the story so many times before. 'Why don't you tell it?' she says. 'Then at least it is over and done with.' She sighs deeply.

'We were not allowed to live here,' her son continues, 'and so we were often harassed by the police. They had already threatened several times to chase us out, when they knocked on the door one evening. "This is it," my mother said. "Quickly, into the closet," my father whispered – and my parents hid themselves in the cupboard. They gave me the key and asked me to lock the door. Instead I opened the front door and told the policemen that they were not at home. For one reason or the other, they left us alone after that. I was nine years old.'

Elizabeth does not really want to be reminded of the story and sighs in relief when it is finished. 'All right,' she says in good spirits and pours water onto the instant coffee. Simon's anecdote, however, appears to be the prologue to a much longer story, which he starts with a simple yet adequate summary of his own personal history: 'Into the closet, out of the closet. That is the story of my life.'

'When I was nineteen years old, I fell in love with a man for the first time. His name was André and he was white. He had placed an advertisement in *Hit*, a youth magazine. He was looking for a black pen pal.' That this veiled term hid a far deeper longing does not detract from the courage of placing such an ad. It was 1977 and any contact across the colour bar, even if this consisted of letters, was forbidden. 'I responded and soon he invited me to come and visit him. He lived in Vanderbijlpark, not far away from here. One day I went and it was love at first sight. But of course I did not mention this to anyone.'

When Nkoli turned twenty, his parents organised a birthday party. It was on this occasion that his mother expressed some doubt. 'He never brought a girlfriend home, like his brother. And he was twenty!' she says. She now seems to have resigned herself to the fact that the rest of the afternoon will be spent reminiscing. 'On my birthday, she said she found my behaviour strange,' her son continues, 'but I did not yet have the courage to confess.'

Some time later Simon and André spent a weekend on the coast.

'He drove me home to Sebokeng in his Mercedes and I got out with my arms full of presents which he had bought for me in Durban. My mother was amazed and yelled: "Don't you have family of your own? Why do you accept all these things from a white man?"'

Elizabeth stares embarrassedly at the floor and says: 'We found such behaviour very strange in those days. We were not used to it.'

Nkoli could only explain his 'strange' behaviour by confessing his relationship with André.

'Elizabeth sat,' he says with a broad smile, 'on top of the same closet. "What did I do to deserve this?" she screamed. "Why is God punishing me? First you get involved in politics and the whole neighbourhood thinks you are a criminal! Now you've come up with something else with which to ruin our reputation. What will the neighbours think? Your grandfather will have a heart attack. How can I explain this to your uncle?"'

Elizabeth gets up, puts the cups on the tray and walks over to the sink.

'My father had no problem with it,' Nkoli continues. 'He worked in the hotel in Vanderbijlpark as a chef. Moffies often stayed there. When he told my mother that, she shouted at him: "Then you are probably like that too."'

It was the start of a tour among the sangomas in the area which took exactly one year. 'It became a matter of making doubly sure,' Nkoli explains, as he continues recalling how he 'came out of the closet'.

'My mother is Christian, but as is the case with so many others, this does not exclude consulting with a traditional healer as a second opinion to the GP. This became a custom because so-called Western doctors were mistrusted under apartheid. At the slightest excuse your leg was amputated. That was cheaper than treatment.'

Years later he seems to be 'completely liberated' from any belief in traditional healers, but initially he too tended to consult with them. 'I also thought that my homosexuality was abnormal.' Thus it was that in 1979 he landed up in front of a female sangoma, together with his mother.

'During our visit she went into a trance and threw bones on the floor. After a while she cried, "He is bewitched!" and after my mother had given her another ten rand, she was willing to part with her knowledge of who was to blame. It appeared to be our neighbour, who is also a sangoma. "It is the thokoloshe," she screeched, "a bad spirit which must be exorcized."'

Elizabeth hunches her shoulders as she rinses the cups and says only: 'That did not really seem likely to me.'

When they accosted the neighbour, they discovered to their amazement that the woman had known for a long time what she was accused of. She had had a dream and she was, quite bluntly, ready to confirm that Nkoli was indeed a homosexual and that his mother could not change this. But that was not the end of the story.

'We went for a second opinion. "He is not sick, but clever," the man said,' as Nkoli remembers. 'And because there was nothing wrong with me, he did not want to accept any money. Then we went for a third opinion.'

Again he was accused of being bewitched, but this time an aunt of his was to blame – a 'diagnosis' that utterly confused Elizabeth. But, a couple of months later and once she had got over the shock, the mother decided to try once again.

'Then we went to a woman who advised us to slaughter a sheep and four chickens and to drink the blood of these animals. "Thanks, but no thanks," I said. After which she whispered in my mother's ear that she would have to boil some eggs, with aloe vera, eucalyptus and my sister's urine.' Nkoli turns up his nose.

In a last desperate effort, Elizabeth sent her son to the minister of her church. 'He read to me from Leviticus 18:22. I could not make head or tail of it but when the man explained, I understood that the Bible said that it was all André's fault, that I had been seduced by a white man to commit sin.'

Eventually it was a psychologist who brought relief. 'One day André's mother phoned mine. First they called each other names because both were convinced that it was the other's fault. But finally they calmed down and André's mother suggested they send us both to a psychologist. She knew one and offered to pay for the treatment. For months on end, André and I visited him every Wednesday afternoon. He made us do tests and had us look at pictures. The one showed a pair of pants and the other a skirt and then he would ask to which I felt most attracted. "To those pants, of course," I said, "because I am a man." Finally he reached a conclusion and said: "Simon, you are one hundred per cent homosexual and the best thing you can do is to accept that. There is nothing wrong with that." After which he asked why André and I would not consider living together.'

That was easier said than done. 'It was 1980 and by living together with André I would break at least two laws: the Group Areas Act and the Immorality Act. "Just pretend you are

André's servant," the psychologist said practically. After which he opened a bottle of champagne and toasted us – and quietly revealed that he was homosexual himself.'

Nkoli's mother could not believe her ears. '"If such a learned man is also a homosexual, then everybody else must be," she said. My father only said: "I told you so."'

Simon Nkoli's homosexuality did not only create conflict with his mother or with widely held beliefs in witches and the healing power of urine. It also challenged his political friends. He got involved at a very young age in the student movement. Even before the Soweto uprising in 1976, he joined the Congress of South African Students (COSAS), a movement that was sympathetic to the banned ANC. Anger over acceptance of a fate with which the older generation appeared to have colluded was combined with a desire for change that set the black townships on fire in the second half of the seventies. 'Freedom in our lifetime' read the prophetic COSAS slogan.

'That you were taught in the language of your oppressor. That you did not have any opportunity to achieve anything. That you were not allowed to live where you wanted. That your parents had been so deeply humiliated for so long. I could no longer take it,' says Nkoli. Within no time, he was appointed regional secretary of the movement in the Transvaal. 'We organised boycotts and protest demonstrations, we pelted the ever-present Casspirs with stones, but we also tried to master the history of the earlier struggle of the ANC before it was banned so as to learn how to transfer blind hatred into viable political ideals and discipline.'

The movement fought for equality, it is true, but when

rumours of Nkoli's homosexuality were doing the rounds within COSAS, it caused a breach.

'A few of my co-executives argued that it was not possible. That it undermined my authority as secretary. According to others, it was alien to our culture. It sounded like an echo from the minister who had tried to convince me that André had converted me. All this was thrown at me during an executive meeting, before I had even "confessed". I hesitated to speak out. When it was decided to call for a general meeting on this issue, I decided to come out of the closet there and then.'

A few weeks later representatives from the different branches met and after the chairperson had opened the meeting, Nkoli got up and confirmed the rumours.

'At first I thought I could get away with a simple "So what?" but when a heavy discussion ensued, I tried to explain. I asked whether there was something wrong with my performance as the organisation's secretary. That was not the case. Then I made it clear that our struggle should not limit itself to the abolition of apartheid. The regime had, after all, also shoved the sodomy laws down our throats, and consequently taken away people's right to be themselves.'

Not everyone was immediately convinced by Nkoli's arguments.

' "Okay, you decide for yourself what lifestyle you want to live," some of my comrades said. "But we are also dealing with a regime that will use this type of thing to discredit you, and with grass-roots support that won't understand." '

'That is true,' I said, 'but now that everyone knows, it is impossible to start rumours about me. And as for those people who don't understand my sexual preference, it should simply be explained to them.'

Eventually Nkoli got the support of eighty per cent of the people present.

When the police opened fire on a group of demonstrators in Sebokeng in September 1984, some people were killed. This drama was repeated a few days later at the funeral of the victims, which was attended by a lot of people. Nkoli and his co-executives, whose task it was as crowd marshals to keep the people's rage from developing into a kangaroo court, could not prevent the hysterical mass of mourners from taking revenge on one particular member of the community. He was suspected of being a police informant and died under a hail of stones.

Nkoli was arrested with twenty-one others and was accused of involvement in the lynching. All in all he spent four years in prison: two years awaiting trial and two years during the trial. In the end, he was released due to lack of evidence. Again, his sexual preference came up and, within the prison walls, stormy debates took place when he acknowledged this to be true.

It all started when it appeared that one of the co-accused had started an affair with another prisoner, a 'common' criminal. This was the gist of a note that fell into Patrick Lekota's hands, the UDF activist who became the natural leader of the twenty-two accused by virtue of his earlier imprisonment on Robben Island. Lekota had made a name for himself on the island as the striker of the prisoners' soccer team. That's where his nickname 'Terror' originated.

Lekota called for an emergency meeting in the biggest cell, cell 47. The case was reported and Lekota explained that such 'excesses' were only grist to the authorities' mill. It should immediately be brought to an end and the person concerned was asked to apologise. So he did.

'I was amazed,' says Nkoli, recalling this particular event. 'When the meeting came to an end and everybody got up to leave, I said in a tiny voice: "And what about me?" The people who had heard what I had said turned around in amazement.

Others asked what I had said, after which I repeated more forcefully: "And what about me?"

'I remember that Father Moselane came up to me, stood in front of me and said: "We have spoken at the same demonstrations. We have lived through so many terrible things together. We are comrades. Comrades. Simon, what are you talking about? You look like a man to me."'

A long consultation followed, which is remembered differently by Nkoli and Lekota. 'Now Patrick alleges that they were only guided by the anxiety that the regime would use my homosexuality against us in the trial – which would not have been the first time that had happened. During the interrogations, my warders made allusions to this. They would take care that I would be raped, they hissed to me. They took all sorts of oblong objects with them to the torture chamber and said: "Why don't you put this in your arse. You like that, don't you?"

'I shared Patrick's fear but said I could not change my sexual preference. So the only thing for me to do was to acknowledge it in public. That reduced the chance of blackmail and gossip. But I still remember clearly that a number of my co-prisoners simply could not accept that I was gay. Patrick himself said that in a democracy, the majority decides on what is good for everybody. Only one or two people took my side. I said: "If you want to, I will stand trial on my own."'

This matter would affect relationships among the twenty-two defendants for months thereafter, until the lawyers of the 'Delmas 22' closed the discussion. They threatened to withdraw if the defendants would not change their attitude towards Nkoli. The many expressions of support from abroad helped convince the men that Nkoli's homosexuality did not threaten solidarity as such.

'On the contrary. For Christmas 1985 I received a hundred and fifty cards, mostly from England and The Netherlands.

Both anti-apartheid movements and gay groups kept me going me all those years.'

Elizabeth nods. Through the agency of the International Defence and Aid Fund, which raised money in London for the defence of political prisoners, she herself received support from a 'lady in Amsterdam' for many years.

Only the Gay Association of South Africa (GASA), which Nkoli had joined in April 1982 as the group's first black member, refused to support his cause. 'They did not want to get involved in politics,' says Nkoli carefully.

GASA, established earlier that year, considered him the proverbial spanner in its apartheid-friendly works. Change your behaviour, play it straight, keep a low profile, do not give offence ... those were the guidelines the executives gave their members and supporters time and again. Then everything would work out in the end.

Nkoli remembers how angry he felt when the organisation refused to show solidarity with a group of lesbians that had been fired in 1983 by their employer, Spoornet.

'For one reason or the other, a considerable number of white dykes worked for the railways. Behind almost every counter at Central Station in Johannesburg you could find one. You could spot them straight away: they conformed to every stereotype people have of dykes – butch, fat and grumpy. One day two lesbians kissed each other on one of the platforms. They were immediately fired, after which almost all the other women went on strike. They were told they could pack their bags too.'

GASA kept silent and when Nkoli insisted on an expression of support, he was told, 'Those dykes asked for it, didn't they?'

Initially Nkoli thought he would be able to force the organisation onto a more progressive track by getting as many black friends as possible to sign up. 'I brought in dozens of new members, but nothing changed.'

In the four years of his imprisonment, none of the GASA executive members ever contacted him. Even worse, they considered him an 'ordinary criminal', judging by a speech of executive member Kevin Botha to a congress of the International Lesbian and Gay Association (ILGA). After Nkoli was released, he understood that GASA members were not simply afraid to be associated with the anti-apartheid activist. 'Most of them were taken in by government propaganda. They saw me as a full-blown terrorist, as a blemish to their organisation. They were just racists, homosexual racists.'

The last straw was an incident during a joint GASA and ILGA trip to a nature reserve. 'The members received an invitation to go for a walk on a Sunday. When I arrived, I was told by an executive member that he was sorry that I could not go inside and that I, together with three black friends, had better wait in the car. The park was "for whites only". When sending the invitations out, it had been forgotten that there were also black members. My friends were too scared to go inside, but I could not care less.'

He got an official reprimand for that. Nkoli resigned his membership. Meanwhile GASA had been expelled from ILGA on account of its refusal to condemn apartheid politics.

'Foreign gay movements wanted GASA to consider black homosexuals as equals and give them executive positions. When they were threatened with expulsion, I was regularly invited to parties by white executive members. And then everyone wanted me to be in a picture with them. Later I heard that they had sent these photos to Europe to create the impression that the organisation was multi-racial. It was pretty obviously fixed and the European gay movements were not convinced,' says Nkoli.

One year after his liberation, he established a new, multiracial gay movement: the Gays and Lesbians of the

Witwatersrand (GLOW), as the area around Johannesburg used to be known. A small number of GASA members switched over to the new organisation, but the majority of the members came from the black townships. Shortly thereafter Nkoli was elected chairperson and Donné Rundle, a white man, was elected secretary.

When we travel back late in the evening to Johannesburg, Nkoli reminisces about the birth of the new movement. 'Within no time we had fifty members! And everybody came to the first meetings. We elected an executive, we opened a PO box, we had strategic planning meetings.'

In the gay circles of the city and Soweto, news of GLOW quickly made the rounds. The international name that Nkoli had gained from his imprisonment was cleverly transformed into foreign financial support. 'In Canada there is a Simon Nkoli Support Group. In Atlanta the mayor declared the fifteenth of September Simon Nkoli Day. In Holland the Dutch gay movement COC and the anti-apartheid movement supported us,' says Nkoli, taking out his wallet. He shows me a picture in which he poses with the African American minister Jesse Jackson. In another photo, he can be seen with Coretta Scott King.

Shortly after its establishment, GLOW thought itself strong enough to proclaim the first Pink Saturday on 5 October 1990.

'I think we were even more encouraged by Nelson Mandela's release and the unbanning of the ANC. In the short term, we would start negotiations. We wanted to make ourselves heard as a gay movement. There was support for our struggle within the ANC, but also resistance. I had already been scolded during many branch meetings. Only if we made ourselves publicly strong and applied the pressure would we be able to get our aims onto the political agenda,' Nkoli says when we get out of the taxi in Pretorius Street.

Skyline is already closed but Connections is still open and here we have a nightcap. Sitting at the bar, Nkoli quickly points out a group of white men. 'The previous GASA executive,' he whispers in my ear. When they see Nkoli, they walk up to him and give him a friendly pat on the back. They congratulate him on the success of the first gay demonstration, creating the impression that they were all active in 'the resistance'. Some want to find out when the next meeting is. One man says he joined GLOW the previous Saturday. His name is Tim and he teaches at a school in Alexandra, a black township north of Johannesburg.

'I hear you are involved in AIDS education,' he says to Nkoli. 'Could I invite you to come to our school so that you can explain safe sex? I mean normally ... neutrally.'

'You mean I can't say that I am gay?'

Tim is silent.

'But sweetie-pie, don't you know that coming out of the closet is my favourite pastime?' Nkoli says.

An unreal silvery-white world, a Côte d'Azur at the southernmost tip of Africa. On this Sunday afternoon an almost endless stream of white pleasure-seekers passes by on the promenade along the Atlantic Ocean: joggers, skateboarders, roller skaters, prams, whining toddlers and happy parents. Nothing seems to be able to disturb their weekend pleasures. The turbulent process of transformation on which the country is embarked and the intensified war between the ANC and Inkatha are a long way away.

Earlier in the day, I had arrived in Cape Town and was met at the airport by an ANC activist whom I had never met, but whom I recognised immediately. Her posture matched the forthrightness which had come through in our earlier telephone conversations, and the slogan 'Nobody knows I'm a lesbian' writ large on her impressive T-shirt quite honestly seemed redundant.

We drove straight to Sea Point. At nerve-racking speed we passed the squatter camps far removed from the city, tens of thousands of huts of cardboard and zinc. Half an hour later, I got out of the car relieved, and when she observed that I was looking a little pale, she only says: 'We do drive a little faster here.'

I learn precious little about her. Her life story is a 'long story' and 'it does not matter,' she says. The issue is that finally the lobbying activities of the Organisation of Lesbian and Gay Activists (OLGA) seem to be getting somewhere (OLGA is a Cape-based lobbying group that was the first to enter into a dialogue on homosexuality with the unbanned ANC).

'We have little time to lose, the negotiations will be starting soon,' she says, stumbling over her own words. She recalls that Foreign Secretary Thabo Mbeki did indeed issue a fine statement in 1988 in which he came out against discrimination on the basis of sexual preference, but whether that point of view is shared by the entire movement she is not yet quite sure.

'If we want the ANC to stick to that policy in the negotiations, we have to exert pressure. I know them inside out – I've been a member for such a long time. Moreover, there is a war going on in one part of the country. Thirty, forty people dead, every weekend in Natal. Here in the townships, the taxi operators are at each other's throats. But the police are behind all that. Part of our leadership is still in prison! I know that it is nonsense, but do you understand that I sometimes feel uncomfortable repeatedly raising "the gay issue" at meetings?'

Then she sums up the support base – the comrades OLGA assumes will support it. 'Tutu is okay, Boesak is okay, we had talks with them. For the rest, all our hope is on Albie.'

ANC executive member Albie Sachs, a lawyer who lost an arm in the 1980s in an attack by a South African death squad in Maputo (Mozambique), has a fine reputation for tabling difficult issues. He had recently told politically committed artists to stop painting clenched fists and singing freedom songs. 'The time has come to practise non-political art,' said Sachs. He also encouraged the movement to engage with environmental issues. 'Freedom is wonderful, but you have to be able to breathe.'

By joining the United Democratic Front (UDF), a coalition of hundreds of organisations and the above-ground arm of the

ANC, OLGA thinks of itself as a mass movement. But four years after its establishment the group still does not count more than six lily-white members.

She wants to know with which ANC leaders in exile I discussed the topic. It feels a bit like telling on someone else, and her tendency to look over her shoulder every so often strengthens the idea of being part of a conspiracy. But it is for a good cause and, after all, I am talking to a real fighter for the resistance. She listens carefully when I tell her how shocked my colleagues in the anti-apartheid movement had been when two ANC executives opposed equal rights in 1987. 'It is about time the majority took over in South Africa. And the majority is against such things,' or so it was according to Solly Smith and Ruth Mompati, who were operating from London. A policy concerning homosexuality? That was abhorrent to Mompati. 'We don't have a policy in the movement for flower sellers, do we?' she told a gay magazine in an interview.

From that moment onwards, we made it a practice as anti-apartheid movement executives to place the issue on the agenda when ANC delegates visited. Something similar happened in the UK, as well as in other European countries. Did it influence Thabo Mbeki's public reprimand of his fellow executives a few months later? That reprimand seemed to provide some relief, but the discussion in the Amsterdam pubs with ANC visitors did not diminish. 'Leather boys, now what are they? Body piercing!? Lesbians who want to adopt daughters?' They had never heard anything quite like it, but felt that 'okay, if we are to consider all of this normal, let's not make an issue out of it.'

During her many visits abroad at the end of the eighties Dutch anti-apartheid movement chairperson Conny Braam made a habit of blowing some of her colleagues' trumpets and then rather pointedly indicating that they were gay. Being gay and a comrade at the same time? Yes, that was possible.

During a conference of South African women in Amsterdam, shortly before Nelson Mandela's release, the subject had come up regularly. When it was mentioned by the exiled ANC Women's League executives that this was all well and good, but that the 'women "at home" were not ready for this yet', some of the representatives burst out laughing. They appeared to be 'women from home'. Some ANC members were so obsessed by the topic that they raised the issue wherever they went.

'But who were these people then?' asks the OLGA activist when we stop at a path leading across the beach to a wall that is a couple of metres high. Diligently, she writes down the names I recollect from my memory.

Every so often a man walks along the pathway to the wall and disappears behind it through a narrow slit. At other times somebody emerges from the slit. On top of the wall there are two tanned bodies. From the bench on the promenade we can easily follow what's going on there.

'That's Graaff's Pool,' she says, having finished writing. 'Officially it was the place where Jewish men could wash and sunbathe naked. Orthodox Jews are not allowed to mix with women during these rituals. But you will have picked up, I'm sure, that it's a cruising spot as well.'

Has it been in existence for a long time?

For years.

Was that allowed?

Yes, it was.

'Once upon a time somebody tried to close it. A woman who lived in a penthouse above one of the apartment buildings behind us laid a charge with the police. Whenever she looked out of her window, she saw naked men, she alleged. Could no one put an end to it? The police investigated and established that she could only see those naked male bodies from a chair on her table.' She laughs, putting her notebook in her bag. We say goodbye near the hotel, not far from the promenade.

In the course of the evening, I cannot resist walking along the promenade again. The Cape Doctor, the strong south-east wind that regularly blows the city clean of smog, makes the waves pound against the rocks. The promenade is still crowded. I sit myself down on the same bench, right in front of Graaff's Pool. Strolling couples pass by, sometimes discreetly looking ahead, at other times staring at the wall that is lit by stadium floodlights. A meeting place very much in the spotlight, Graaff's Pool does not hide its secrets.

There is a coming and going of men. Sometimes an inquisitive woman fails to suppress her curiosity. 'Stop doing that,' her husband appears to tell her. 'Come on, why don't you let me?' says the wife and walks along the pathway to the wall. Then she reads the text on the sign next to the entrance and thereafter she quickly glances through the slit. One woman walks away shaking her head, while another one calls her husband – but he does not care to join her.

After one hour the couples have all but disappeared and only men stay behind. They seem to be walking up and down aimlessly and keep loitering near the gate at the end of the path. A silent world where a glance can lead to a short romance.

It is getting late when I finally pluck up the courage to penetrate beyond the wall. Slowly I walk along the pathway and when I arrive at the entrance, I read: 'Men only'. As I take a peek inside, more than a dozen eyes peer at me searchingly.

From my hotel room in Cape Town I can see Robben Island. A thin strip in the ocean. When the weather is good, you can see the lighthouse. In October 1990 there are still hundreds of political prisoners and 'common' criminals incarcerated there. The minority government has, of course, committed to releasing them, but first of all the prisoners have to undergo a time-consuming bureaucratic process and sign a statement – a statement that comes close to an admission of guilt. Every couple of weeks a boat arrives in Cape Town harbour and a few newly free and undoubtedly happy people clamber ashore.

Three days in a row, my day begins with the opening of the curtains and long moments spent staring at that island. Every so often pleasure boats sail across my view, and when my stare moves away from the island, my gaze falls on bungalows, more hotels and penthouses. A strange contrast. In the same way, the joggers thronging the boulevard and the blond surfers cresting the waves represent the world of Peter Stuyvesant cigarettes, while just a few kilometres away lies the very different world of Nelson Mandela.

It was the Portuguese explorer Vasco da Gama who, as the first European to sight these shores, put Robben Island on the world map. He did not find any humans there, only seals and penguins. Subsequent English sailors named the island after the

Dutch word (*robbe*) for the former of the two species. That pirates were really boys who sometimes longed for their mothers when quartering and keelhauling people is apparent from the fact that Dutchman Joris van Spilbergen renamed the island after his mother Isla de Cornelia at the beginning of the seventeenth century. It was the crew of the *Oranje* that eventually declared the island to be Robben Island in 1608 and, in celebration, they clobbered a hundred seals to death. For fun, not food, that being the prerogative of Scandinavian buccaneers who cooked and served the seals with prunes and honey.

In the early days Robben Island was used merely as a 'poste restante' by international seafarers – a place to stop on the way east or west to pick up messages left by others. Meanwhile, on the mainland, someone had set up a refreshment station for the very same ships. A quick cup of hot soup and a glass of brandied raisins – that was the start of over three hundred years of white domination, launched by the genocide perpetrated on the original inhabitants of the country, the Khoi-Khoi.

How Robben Island developed from postbox to South African Alcatraz requires some explanation at this point. The reason was Harry the Strandloper. This young Khoi man's real name was Autshumato, and he had lived for over eight years on the island before the Dutch East India Company's employees colonised the Cape. He was taken there at his own request, with about sixty followers, by a passing English ship. He had probably been fighting with other Hottentots, as the Khoi are known in colonial history. Perhaps the tension had arisen because Harry had slowly but surely 'anglicised' himself – the man even paraded around in European clothes – and he also took advantage of every British visit to learn the language.

After his return to the mainland in 1640, he earned a good living as a translator between the Khoi and the English sailors. He maintained this role after the arrival of Jan van Riebeeck in

1652. For the VOC employee, English was as just as much gobbledegook as it was for the original inhabitants of the area – and the Hollanders were mighty suspicious of anything that Harry might be cooking up with the Brits. Thus, it is on account of this Strandloper that Van Riebeeck introduced the idea (in his journal of November 1652) of turning Robben Island into a prison.

Harry himself managed to prevent his deportation for the next six years, but eventually he had no choice. Almost a year after his detention, he succeeded in escaping from Robben Island by rowing boat. His fate beyond that is unknown.

This is the beginning of a sad history. The 'Bandit Rolls' in the Cape Archives are painful proof of the Dutch drive to rid their colonies of political troublemakers. Thus, over the centuries, rebellious slaves and defiant 'Burghers' were put to work in the quarries on Robben Island. Accompanying them were 'Indians' from East India, such as the Prince of Macassar, who was taken there with a servant in 1682, and the Prince of Ternate, who met the same fate in 1728. Furthermore, the island was home to the Princes of Madagascar and Madura, as well as to Muslim leaders such as Hadji Mattarm, whose grave can still be located on the island.

After the British took over the government of the Cape Province from the Dutch at the beginning of the nineteenth century, Robben Island became the place of exile for rebellious black leaders such as Chief Langalibalele, Chief Maqoma and the Xhosa prophet Nxele, who had led an attack on Grahamstown, a town colonised by the British in 1819. From time to time Robben Island was also used as place of detention for lepers and the mentally disturbed.

Occasionally a 'sodomite' was sent into exile on the island. The Bandit Rolls from the eighteenth century tell us the heart-rending story of Rijkhaart Jacobz, a red-haired Rotterdammer who arrived at Robben Island in 1713. Jacobz had been sentenced to twenty-five years of exile for a crime that 'could not be named'. After his arrival, he was immediately put up in the Bandit House, which, although made only from twigs and mud plaster, had a view of the Atlantic Ocean. Some months later four additional prisoners arrived: Manaij of Boegies, Klaas of Kus Malaba, Petrus Malgas and Klaas Blank. These Khoi had been sentenced to fifty years in exile on account of theft.

Rijkhaart Jacobz and Klaas Blank, a short, coffee-coloured young man of about twenty, got to know each other in the quarry. How a romance developed from that first meeting is not recorded, but we can take a guess. It wasn't long before Rijkhaart and Klaas started having supper together in the evening and after a while – we're talking real love here, the sort where two people get to know each other first before sharing a bed – it happened. In the Bandit House.

Probably because Klaas traded in dagga, which the warders were particularly fond of, the two of them were allowed to build their own hut on Robben Island's beach. They lived there for twenty years and, after their daily forced labour, made passionate love. It did not matter to the chief warden, Sergeant Scholtz, who had an affair with a freed slave himself. As long as the crime remained 'unnamed'.

Many years later, due to a tragic chain of events, the affair between Rijkhaart Jacobz and Klaas Blank came to an abrupt end. In the first place, their heterosexual co-prisioners, driven by jealousy – why are those two allowed to live in a hut of their own and not us? – started to gossip. Manaij of Boegies, for instance, could not find his fishing net one day in 1735 and soon the rumour did the rounds that Jacobz had stolen it. When Boegies confronted him on the issue, the Rotterdammer allegedly dropped his pants and touched his private parts. It was this event that reminded the slave Augustijn Matthisz that he had seen the two 'in action' in their hut eleven years before, 'perpetrating a terrible sin'. Prisoners went off to find Sergeant Scholtz and ratted on the two. He did not show any interest, but when he retired and left the island some time later, the jealous men took their chance. They found a more sympathetic ear with his successor, Godlieb Willer. The deeply religious overseer did not let the matter pass. Initially Jacobz denied all accusations. He had been drunk when Matthisz had seen him with Blank. And he was only naked because his pants had accidentally fallen down. But after a severe hiding with a sjambok, he confessed. 'Don't hit me! I did it. Send me to the courthouse,' Jacobz shouted.

'The prisoners confess on all points' is what the register tells us. On 18 August 1735 Jacobz and Blank were sentenced to death. Chained to each other and dressed only in their prison pants, a ship took them out into the ocean a few days later and they were thrown to the sharks.

After Robben Island had harboured only 'common' criminals in the first half of the twentieth century, the apartheid government resumed the old tradition in 1961. With Nelson Mandela's exile, initially for five years but extended to life-long imprisonment in 1964, Robben Island again became a dumping ground for political opponents. In one sense it was an enormous miscalculation. The remote island appealed to the imagination of a growing international movement that opposed apartheid policy. During his imprisonment, Mandela became the symbol of resistance from within the country. The simple fact that men whose only crime was a desire to destroy institutionalised racism in their own country were incarcerated on the island was sufficient to make every desperate attempt at reform in the 1980s by President P.W. Botha (nicknamed 'die Groot Krokodil') fail. 'Liberation first!' was the battle-cry.

'I saw it as a university,' says Jabulani Mbandla, a student leader sentenced to six years in prison after the Soweto uprising in 1976. Just sixteen years old, he was the youngest prisoner ever to be sent to Robben Island. 'Of course I dreaded going there, but on the other hand I also looked forward to it. In any case, there was no longer any torture. Before that I had, all in all, spent three years in solitary confinement. I had been interrogated many times. Then a rope was wrapped around my arm, with a stone attached to it. I was given electric shocks. On the boat to Robben Island, I realised that all of that was now behind me – that the treatment would be better there because all international attention was focused on the island,' says Mbandla.

A certain excitement was also caused by the fact that he would meet the leadership on the island: Madiba and Tata (as Mandela and Sisulu were called), Govan Mbeki, and Ahmed Kathadra. Mbandla is still very proud of and grateful for the opportunity the six-year period gave him to completely master the ANC's ideals.

'Outside, our defiance was inspired by anger. Our actions were uncoordinated, we were loose cannons. Only on the island did I learn what the true purpose of our struggle was: the creation of a non-racial South Africa. It was not a struggle against whites per se, but against apartheid politics. On Robben Island I came to realise why, despite my ambitions, I was denied all opportunity to get ahead.

'*Who's to be Blamed?* was the name of a play I saw in school. My parents were not to blame. Nor was my environment. It was the system that held us back. That is what I was taught on the island.' The small man behind the over-large desk at the development organisation for which he now works derives his present status from his years on Robben Island. He sees himself as a leader. 'I cooked for Mandela,' he says with a smile.

Mbandla shared a cell with twenty-six others. With one of them he started an affair. 'I don't think that he was homosexual, rather a lack of women seduced him to respond to my advances.' Mbandla suspects that a few fellow-prisoners suspected something, but they never discussed it. 'We slept side by side on the floor and only when it was completely dark did we embrace each other.'

Wasn't it terrible that everything had to take place in secret, that he could not come out with it? 'Not at all,' says Mbandla, sitting on the edge of his chair. 'The Robben Island leadership represented a high morality. Today these are the people who make the laws in the country. There was an iron discipline on Robben Island. After all, we had to set the example and had to distinguish ourselves from the ordinary criminals. On the island we tried to create the type of society of which we dreamt – in a small way and under impossible circumstances. Everything was tightly organised. The old leaders gave lectures. Amongst ourselves, we elected therapists, teachers, representatives for sport and entertainment. We were aware that we had to be examples of decency to all.'

But isn't that impossible as a homosexual? Mbandla shakes his head. 'Our leadership's resistance to homosexuality was understandable. Not on account of culture or tradition but on account of the low morality of most gays. They use drugs, are always drunk: "F and F, fun and fuck". That behaviour disgusts people.'

'Many heterosexual men in Soweto, however, also have affairs and are sitting behind their first beer at nine o'clock on Sunday morning,' I say.

'Exactly, but we form a minority – and if we want to be accepted, we have to behave ourselves.' Mbandla feels that the gay movement should be less concerned with parades and parties and should focus on the 're-education' of homosexuals as respectable citizens. I begin to suspect he is ashamed of his sexual preference. 'It is no shame,' he says carefully, 'but it is true that I have acquired my homosexuality in the struggle. The action groups in Soweto, the police cells, Robben Island – I always lived in a male world. When I was liberated, I tried to build a normal family life. I married and we had two children. Look, here they are,' says Mbandla, showing a few pictures. 'But I could not, I was not able to. Both the struggle and my imprisonment took away my youth. I never went out, never played soccer. That's why.'

At the end of the conversation he grabs his diary and some files and puts them in his briefcase. Tonight he will fly to Durban for work. 'To the beach, lekker,' I say. 'I have seen enough ocean for the rest of my life,' he retorts.

❦❦❦

The modern corset into which the men who eventually led their country to the abolition of apartheid laced themselves, must have forced some who were comrades and also gay into periods of breathtaking loneliness. Witness to that is the story of Indres Pillay, who was banished to the island in 1989, shortly before Nelson Mandela's release, and left it two years later. Pillay was involved in the underground activities of the ANC. He does not want to talk about it any more, but some of his memories have been published in the Dutch *Anti-Apartheidskrant*:

'The political prisoners had mutually agreed on a code of conduct. One of the rules was that "anti-social behaviour" was not allowed. It took a while before I realised what this meant, but later on it became clear to me that that referred to homosexual activities. "Only the prisoners of the PAC practise 'anti-social' behaviour," I was told in private once. Later I even discovered that that was not strictly true: there were also some cases of gay "activity" between ANC prisoners.'

Nevertheless, as Pillay has written, there was an atmosphere of 'perestroika' on the island. Everyone – prisoners as well as warders – felt that things were about to change. Thus it was that prisoners were allowed to read newspapers and hire videos. 'At a certain moment there was some sort of order from the leadership of the ANC island group that nobody was allowed to watch films with gay scenes, whether between men or women. This order followed the screening of the film *9 1/2 Weeks*, in which there is a very short scene of two women who embrace passionately. Apparently this scene had seriously shocked some prisoners. In order to test this homophobic attitude, I asked for *Kiss of the Spiderwoman* to be screened. I was asked what the film was about and said: "About a relationship in prison between a revolutionary and a sympathiser." Everybody seemed very enthusiastic about the theme, and the film was ordered. Of course I had not mentioned the gay character of the relationship between the two protagonists in their prison cell. When the film was shown in section B, where the ANC leadership usually hung out, there was first of all a stunned silence, followed by the shriek: "Stop this movie! It is anti-social."'

Pillay protested against this form of censorship. 'I said that I was entitled to my freedom of choice, and that I had been incarcerated because I had fought for these basic rights, against an oppressive system. And I questioned why we had to apply self-censorship while being forced to live in an environment censored by the enemy? The discussion ended when everybody left the auditorium and I was left behind on my own to watch a movie that I had already seen.'

While Indres Pillay finally came to identify with somebody from another cell who felt the same as he did, elsewhere in the world his comrades had turned their back on him.

Eventually his co-prisoners reacted more positively to his knitting activities. 'Somebody who came to visit me had given me the idea to start knitting, because you have to do something to stave off the tensions and boredom of prison life. Together with another prisoner, also a liberated spirit, I started knitting. The others looked at us and shook their heads. Knitting meant that you were gay or that you were not really aware of the differences between male and female activities. After I had knitted some jerseys and shawls in the ANC colours – they were beautiful, if I might say so – they started to change their opinion. And after some time there was an active knitting club on the island. This was some sort of victory, albeit a minor one.'

Summer 1993. After three rings there is still no answer. The day before my departure for South Africa, to remind him, I had told Simon Nkoli the arrival time of my flight, but he is not at home when I arrive. Called away to an urgent meeting, out doing some last-minute shopping, who knows? I wait with my two suitcases in the lobby of the apartment block in Hopkins Street, Yeoville, to which he has recently moved. The hot sun burns my face as I flip through the newspaper. The negotiations between the ANC and the National Party seem to be on a collision course yet again. The former strives towards the drafting of a new constitution by an elected legislative group. The latter wants to leave this to representatives of all political parties, including those whose support base is doubtful – and they want it to happen behind closed doors. Both sides are deeply and seemingly immovably entrenched.

After fifteen minutes, Paul comes running up to me. Simon's housemate, a minister of the gay church in Hillbrow, wipes the sweat from his forehead as he picks up one of my suitcases. 'Sorry, but I've just come from the hospital,' he says apologetically. 'It happened yesterday morning. When he was washing up, Simon's knees suddenly gave way. He started sweating heavily. He couldn't get up. He was foaming at the mouth,' Paul slowly recalls, with tears in his eyes. Together with a few friends he had taken Simon to hospital where he was instantly admitted. This morning his condition seemed to have changed very little. 'He is hardly able to move and has a very high fever. His memory has been affected. Don't let it be …' We don't say another word for some time.

'Perhaps it's pneumonia. Perhaps he's burnt out,' I try.

'Let's hope it's that.' Paul does not seem to be comforted.

Slowly I unpack my suitcases. Paul neatly puts my clothes away in the closet of the spare bedroom. I put the alarm clock next to my bed, shoes under the desk. I leave the two brand-new dildoes in my suitcase for the time being. I page through a number of documents, background material for the articles that I have to write. Reports from a country that stumbles towards an uncertain future. But this afternoon I don't seem to be able to focus …

When Paul returns from a visit to the hospital in the early evening, he appears suddenly relieved and happy. 'Everything's under control,' he says. 'It's TB … just TB. The doctor says it's not without risk, but they will get him through.'

In the next couple of days, things gradually improve. The sweating stops, his memory slowly returns. 'I thought I was done for,' says Simon Nkoli when I visit him in the hospital a week later, 'but it's TB and I'm lucky not to have had it for too long; it was discovered at an early stage. Medication and rest should get me back on my feet within a couple of months, my doctor says. And if that doesn't work, I'll just visit a sangoma.' He laughs at his own joke, his face full of pain.

Hardly reassured, I prepare to file my first report.

When it comes to health issues, eighty per cent of the black population of South Africa first consults a sangoma. But it's not only blacks that rely on the advice of tens of thousands of 'witch doctors' in this country. In some areas of South Africa, 'Western' doctors co-operate with the healers, and rumour has it that even ex-president P.W. Botha has consulted with a private sangoma in Soweto from time to time. Since the AIDS epidemic seems set to disrupt severely the birth of a free and democratic South Africa, sex education organisations set great store on appealing to those who have the people's ears – in other words, the sangomas.

▽▽▽

It is always hot in the kingdom of Modjadji, the rain queen of Tzaneen in the northern Transvaal. Yet almost everyone in the region at the foot of the Drakensberg is convinced that the woman is able to make rain. Mysticism plays a big part in the world of the Shangaan, one of the black tribes of South Africa. It also accounts for the substantial presence of traditional healers in this once semi-independent homeland of Gazankulu, where the Shangaan people were herded together in line with the old apartheid legislation. The regional organisation of sangomas has over two thousand members, and there are many more that have not joined up. In some villages every family has its own sangoma.

However, the situation is not unique to this area. Traditional healers are found all over the country, in urban as well as rural areas. The fifty thousand or so sangomas that practise throughout the country are represented by nearly twenty organisations which are petitioning for the recognition of traditional healing by the government and its health department.

Research shows that a sangoma treats on average over twenty patients per week, which is approximately one thousand per year. Traditional healers themselves, and many of their clients, are convinced of the healing effect of their treatment. It is believed that one can tell what the patient's problem is by throwing a bag of bones and reading them. Once in a trance, it is said, one can contact the ancestors, who give the treatment advice. Much use is also made of medicinal herbs. In some cases

– for instance, in the case of compound fractures – referral to a hospital takes place, but in cases such as venereal disease, epilepsy, hypertension, cancer or psychological problems, it is believed that sangomas have enough knowledge to prescribe treatment.

The official health-care system is – together with a fair chunk of the black population – very sceptical of the sangomas' ability to cure anything. Officials of the sangoma organisations recognise that there are a lot of quacks about and that some traditional healers are motivated purely by competition, old-fashioned prejudice and the simple desire to make a fast buck. But recognition of the true value of traditional medicine could put an end to those practices, they say.

Dr Nthato Motlana, a well-respected doctor from Soweto, is, however, highly sceptical. 'Sangomas,' he says, 'base their judgement on the throwing of bones and on what they have dreamt. That is not a diagnosis – it is deceit. They claim to uphold an African tradition, but there is nothing African about traditional healing, as it can be found all over the world. No more than conventional medicine should be dismissed as "Western". State-of-the-art medicine is the result of two hundred years of research across the globe, and draws from research and customs from all over the world, including Africa.' According to Motlana, people turn to sangomas for no other reason than the lack of access to sound health-care provision.

For the time being, Doctor Motlana is a voice crying in the wilderness. The popularity of sangomas has increased in direct proportion to the distrust of the black population in the inferior health-care system set up by the white minority government. According to Dingaan Ndlovu, chairperson of the regional organisation of traditional healers in Gazankulu, sangomas owe their authority specifically to the fact that they 'do not amputate immediately' in case of wounds to specific parts of the body. 'That was the rule rather than the exception in the case of state health care,' according to Ndlovu.

Meanwhile the HIV virus spreads throughout the country infecting at least 1600 people per day, according to researchers. The heartening observation that the prevalence among white homosexuals is reasonably under control is completely overshadowed by the rapid growth of the number of HIV-positive cases among black heterosexuals and homosexuals – and, more specifically, women.

In the bleakest prognoses, it is estimated that there are over four million seropositive people in South Africa – about ten per cent of the population. And it is expected that the virus will spread faster here than anywhere else in Africa because there is a very mobile workforce in comparison with other African countries – and hundreds of thousands of people live and work far from their families and therefore resort to unsafe sex. The prediction that young, highly educated blacks will be severely hit by the disease is similarly frightening.

'I am afraid that by the time everybody recognises the disastrous consequences of AIDS for this country, it will be too late,' says Bongi Zonkwe. A staff member for AIDSCOM/AIDSCAP, an American sex education NGO, she is conducting a workshop for one hundred fifty sangomas in Nkowankowa township near Tzaneen. Yet she is positive about the work of her organisation, which views traditional healers as a bridge to the black masses.

'The campaign got off the ground in September 1992 with a national workshop for about thirty healers. The idea is that they train thirty others within a period of six months. This workshop is part of that first phase. Ideally speaking, we would have trained about nine hundred healers, and after a year, thirty times as many – twenty-seven thousand, more than half the total number. It probably won't happen that fast, but participation is encouraging.'

Zonkwe finds a remarkable openness with respect to 'curiosities' such as dildoes and condoms. 'In the Shangaan tradition, women are not allowed to see the penis, but during the workshop we noticed that this tradition is put aside, when health is endangered.' There is, however, a lot of giggling during the meetings.

Zonkwe is convinced the workshops are effective: 'Most sangomas take the dildoes and condoms home to demonstrate their use to their clients.'

During the course, a lot of attention is also given to the dangers of infection via blood. The healers are advised to use rubber gloves. Sangomas regard AIDS as a disease caused by 'bad blood'. 'We tell them that the white blood cells in the body are soldiers, who are being guarded by higher-ranking officers, the T-cells. Due to unsafe sex, the enemy, the HIV virus, sneaks into the body and passes the soldiers in disguise. The enemy murders the officers and puts on their uniforms. The soldiers are misled in that way, follow the instructions of the enemy in disguise and allow even more enemies to penetrate the body. Within a short period of time the entire body is controlled by the enemy and AIDS develops,' Zonkwe explains. In a role-play, sangomas are subsequently asked to treat somebody with AIDS. 'From that role-play we learned that they see the symptoms caused by the virus as something that has to do with thokoloshe, a bewitched ancestral ghost, which infects the blood. People with AIDS are advised to have no sex with others. However, one can also get advice on how the client can deal with discrimination and possible unemployment.'

Unsafe sex is, in any case, very broadly interpreted by traditional healers. Sex after abortion is forbidden, as is having an affair. Likewise, widows are dissuaded from having sex in the first year of mourning. Anal sex with women, blowjobs and gay sex are taboo in the eyes of many sangomas, although it is acknowledged that 'evil' is everywhere and this is often dealt with in very practical ways. AIDSCOM/AIDSCAP makes use of the opportunity to challenge prejudices which are often felt to be traditional.

❦❦❦

Dr Motlana sees the continued existence of traditional forms of treatment as a potential cause of further spread of the virus. After all, many healers make use of dirty knives – for instance, for circumcision – and are in constant contact with blood. 'Moreover,' says Motlana, 'they only too often create the impression of being able to cure AIDS. At the moment the story is doing the rounds that there is a small plant in southern Natal that, when picked at the right moment, would be able to cure the disease. This is very dangerous nonsense, which prevents people from practising safe sex.'

Bongi Zonkwe, on the other hand, suggests we need to accept the sangomas as a reality: 'There is plenty of evidence to prove that they are indeed able to heal people.' Everything must therefore be put into place to urge people to have safe sex. 'And for the time being, our workshops have more effect than government brochures in which AIDS is represented as a "black disease".'

The young Shangaan men with their beautifully painted faces and brightly coloured attire have made a deep impression on me. With a mixture of courage and despair I force myself to control my fantasies. Here is a culture I am not familiar with and I hate the urge prevalent among homosexuals to see everyone else as potentially gay. It would, in this case, be blatant wishful thinking and would also constitute a severe case of Eurocentric thinking: they put on make-up, they put on dresses, they constantly touch each other's bodies ... well, then, there's only one conclusion.

'But they are often moffies,' Simon says when I tell him about my trip to Tzaneen. 'That's how culture solves the problem. If you behave in a very feminine manner, then a female ancestor has apparently descended into you. And if you represent the wisdom of the ancestors, then you will become a sangoma.'

We are in Ron and Stephen's garden: Stephen is ophthalmologist to both Nelson Mandela and Eugene Terre'blanche. After Simon had been discharged from hospital, they offered Simon the opportunity to recover at their impressive home. The couple joined the ANC recently and they are by no means the only gays in this plush suburb.

After the maid has served tea, Simon softly says: 'So they thought it was only TB, but my GP didn't trust their diagnosis. He retrieved my medical files from the police. It became clear that I had been tested for AIDS while in detention. So I was HIV as far back as 1985.'

He stares at the tennis court and sighs deeply.

'They constantly said so, during the interrogations. "You are sick, boy, you've got AIDS. Why don't you admit having killed that sell-out, you don't have long to live anyway." But I never believed a word they said. I thought they were only trying to intimidate me. Now it appears they tested me secretly. The scum.'

After this discovery, the GP had a new test done. 'Apparently I have one cell left.' Simon then asks me to keep the news to myself. 'I am still too tired to shout it from the rooftops. To come out of the closet again; to explain that I am gay *and* HIV, and that that is no reason for being envious of me. I'll get round to it. So I've been HIV for at least eight years and I intend to break all records. Out of the closet, into the coffin ... but not yet. I first want to experience it all: the first democratic elections, Mandela's inauguration, a constitution that guarantees the right of sexual freedom. After that, we'll take it from there.'

❦❦❦

Shortly afterwards, the country comes close to total chaos after the murder of the almost mythical ANC leader Chris Hani in April 1993. Suddenly the National Party is prepared to make far-reaching compromises. Its new, moderate top negotiator, Roelf Meyer, agrees to an election date as well as to the establishment of an elected constitutional assembly.

Two white faces among thousands of black ones. In the Soweto stadium a memorial service takes place for Chris Hani. When the masses rise to sing the ANC anthem, the young white man waves the flag of the South African Communist Party. The woman next to him clenches her fist.

Johan and Elsabé are from Pretoria. This is their first political rally. When we leave the stadium after the service and bump into each other, we start talking. 'It is not scary, it is strange,' says Elsabé, who has never been in the presence of so many blacks before. 'Where we live, everybody is white, Afrikaans. It is as if we've arrived in a different world.'

The two of them joined the ANC a year before. It is a deep family secret. Their parents are also unaware of Johan's homosexuality, as they are of the fact that sister Suzette has a relationship with her female 'housemate'.

'We live in a cocoon of lies,' says Elsabé. 'We pile the one excuse on top of the other and hope not to contradict each other. Like I told my mother yesterday that I was going to make a trip to the Magaliesberg today. Let's just hope we won't be seen on TV.'

'They could murder us for it,' continues Johan. 'When I confessed to my father years ago that the whole apartheid system might as well be done away with as far as I was concerned, he chased after me with a gun. I slept in a park that night and only dared go home after two weeks.'

Elsabé understands why Johan's confession was such a disappointment to her parents, who have been members of the

Dutch Reformed Church all their lives. 'Johan joined the Voortrekkers Youth Brigade as all good boys were expected to. Afterwards, he joined the Afrikaner Weerstandsbeweging,' his sister discloses. 'This had nothing to do with racism,' Johan says, 'but rather an unshakeable belief in Afrikaner culture. Helped, perhaps, by a slight fantasy for uniforms.'

Things changed when it became clear to him that that culture 'entailed very little else but boerewors and brandy and Coke. I discovered that almost all great Afrikaans writers turned against apartheid and that at youth festivals, in the latter half of the 1980s, Koos Kombuis and Johannes Kerkorrel performed to lyrics that likewise expressed a loathing of white supremacy. I realised I was on completely the wrong track.'

As we reach the exit from the stadium, we end up behind the GLOW banner. 'Gays and Lesbians support the struggle for a non-racial, democratic South Africa,' I read.

'We are also involved in establishing a gay movement in Pretoria,' says Johan. 'Tonight we are going to distribute pamphlets in the gay bars.'

'Gay bars in Pretoria?'

'More than that,' Johan says proudly. 'There are two gay churches and a sauna as well!'

'Pretoria has, relatively speaking, the largest number of single households in South Africa,' Elsabé adds.

Shame!

every time I catch up with eleven-year-old Kari, huffing and puffing and desperately trying to catch my breath, he says: 'And now we must move on.' Keeping up this punishing pace, the diminutive black guide discloses the secrets of the immense, centuries-old ruins of Great Zimbabwe which rise up out of the plain in an area called Masvingo. The king's chambers at the top of the hill; the servants' kraal; the ramparts, erected to keep the Matabele out; a lookout; the seven famous stone-carved birds which centuries ago were taken home as souvenirs by colonial tourists.

Long ago, sometime between the thirteenth and eighteenth centuries, this was the headquarters of a mighty kingdom stretching deep into Mozambique and Botswana. In the modest museum, a few tin objects and some pieces of jewellery that the colonial visitors overlooked remind one of a once prosperous economy that was based partly on barter with tradesmen from the East and partly on gold mining. And all this long before white travellers created the 'first' trade routes and British adventurers claimed to have 'discovered' gold in their Rhodesia.

Chest puffed out and hands in his pockets, Kari scans the horizon: a wild and rugged landscape that erupted hundreds of thousands of years ago from the trembling earth. A rock blanket covers this land which derived its new name from these ruins after independence: Zimbabwe, house of stones. These stones have simply been placed on top of each other, without cement. 'If you pull one out, the whole structure collapses,' Kari smiles. Then we have to move on, to Watergate down below, which once provided access to a waterway, which is now merely a parched riverbed. Then we're off uphill again. A completely cloudless sky offers no shelter from the burning heat.

'He who is without sin shall cast the first stone.' It was the Gays and Lesbians of Zimbabwe (GALZ) who shook the shaky structure of modern Zimbabwe for the first time. After six years the executive committee of this till then lily-white social club realised that the moment had come to hide no longer behind a PO box address in Harare. People felt encouraged by developments in South Africa, where a fast-growing gay and lesbian movement had succeeded in putting freedom of sexual orientation high on the agenda of the negotiators of the new constitution. Financially supported by Hivos, a Dutch NGO, the organisation registered for the annual Zimbabwe Book Fair, the largest in Africa, with the intention of distributing folders and brochures. It was time to call a spade a spade.

When President Mugabe got wind of this plan, he exploded. GALZ was prohibited access after the government threatened to withdraw its financial support for the fair. 'They are lower than dogs and pigs, for these animals don't know homosexual behaviour,' the President said in his opening address to the participants. He referred to GALZ as an 'association of perverts and sodomites'. One week later, in a speech to a delegation of the Women's League of governing party ZANU-PF, which, due to the President's many foreign visits, seems to be permanently resident at the airport, he added to this insult by encouraging the population to take the law into its own hands, to arrest homosexuals, to report and deport them. Homosexuality was 'un-African and in conflict with black culture', according to Mugabe.

When, a couple of weeks later, I drive into the village of Gwanda on my way to Harare, I see two men walking hand in hand in the street. In the local hotel a friendly waiter urges me to go with him to the local nightclub. Here Jonas, a mineworker, asks me to dance with him ... until Harrington pushes him away, pulls me to the middle of the dance floor and elicits cheering from the crowd with a startling demonstration of dirty dancing. Harrington likes me apparently, and although it is very late and I have to be on my way to the capital early the next morning, we start talking in a dark corner, his hand on my leg. When I ask him whether he is gay, he vehemently shakes his head in denial. 'But,' he says, 'I would like to join you in your hotel.'

▼▼▼

I am looking for Anthony, whom I got to know a year earlier in a gay bar in Johannesburg. He had travelled temporarily to South Africa, found a job as a tailor, and in his spare time enjoyed the freedom that South Africa then offered, shortly before the first democratic elections. He was twenty-one at the time, black, beautiful and had a sense of humour. In April 1994 he returned to Zimbabwe to finish his course in clothing design. Until a few months before, we had kept in contact by telephone, but now the phone goes unanswered. Not unusual in this country where lines go dead every so often, numbers change overnight and people are constantly on the move. But after President Mugabe's call for the reporting and deporting of homosexuals, I felt somewhat concerned. Where could he be?

After a trip through Zimbabwe's nature reserves, a barren and dry savannah landscape, I finally arrive in Harare. Steven, a white friend, immediately tells me that Anthony has moved house. On our way to the church of the Salvation Army, where

Anthony plays the organ, I am brought up to speed on the latest developments. The anti-homosexual tirades on television and in the newspapers have given way to continuous praise for the All Africa Games. 'But in both cases the idea is to distract people from the drought and the people in Matabeleland who are dying of hunger,' says Steven. He is considering emigrating to Australia, where a sister of his lives, and all his white gay friends are thinking the same way. 'We live in fear.'

At seven, church is over and Anthony comes walking out. We embrace. No, I can't stay in the hotel: I must come and stay with him. In the former maid's quarters I finally find some rest after a tiring trip, nestling next to Archibald, the teddy bear. Anthony practises the organ: 'Onward Christian Soldiers'!

'Aren't you at risk after Mugabe's speech?' I ask.

'Not yet. But I am not afraid. I hear ministers in my church ape the President. But meanwhile ...'

'Are there many gay churchgoers and ministers?'

'Hundreds of them!'

'Have you come out of the closet?'

'Oh no!' he screams at his most effeminate. 'On Sunday I go to church twice. I say a friendly hello to everyone, I attend the service and play the organ. After service, I leave straightaway. Everyone is talking about family matters, about children. I have nothing to contribute. Sometimes you land up in a conversation like that anyway, when someone says: "Do you know that so and so is a homosexual?" and then I say: "Really?"'

Anthony thinks that nobody suspects that he is gay. 'But the way you walk and talk, isn't that a give-away?' I say.

'To you it is, but not here,' Michael says defensively. After which he starts up with 'A Safe Stronghold Our God is Still'.

Mugabe's attack draws, it is true, fierce responses from a large number of publishers present at the book fair in July 1995, from internationally renowned authors like Nigerian Wole Soyinka and South African Nadine Gordimer, from Archbishop Tutu, from international support organisations ... but in his own country the President receives almost unanimous support. The ministers present at the opening ceremony of the fair practically peed in their pants with laughter during his speech. The delegation of the Anglican Women's League, to which Mugabe appealed a couple of days later, also cooed with laughter. During a hastily convened meeting of Parliament, in which Mugabe's party occupies 149 out of 150 seats (an intricate election system excludes almost any form of opposition in Zimbabwe), one after the other member parroted the President. Only one of the members expressed some form of doubt. 'How will we explain to our voters that we talked about homosexuality for hours in Parliament?' the man quipped.

With just one exception, the newspaper editors praised the President for his 'courageous attack'. That one exception argued that Zimbabwe should leave its homosexuals alone as long as they didn't break the law and have sex in the streets, 'like in San Francisco or Amsterdam'.

The absence of the gay movement at the fair was symbolised by an empty table on which, in the course of the following days, flowers and letters of sympathy were placed. A poster in Shona, the most widely spoken indigenous Zimbabwean language, was personally torn up by the Minister of Home Affairs. At some distance from the table, gay activists talked furtively with passers-by. During a public discussion, some young black men and women openly admitted their homosexuality. They were the only ray of hope.

The day after my arrival, I was told at the former office of GALZ that the organisation's archives had been transferred to a safe house. There was only the postbox address left and Beverley, who runs a curio shop next to the office, claimed that she was no longer active in GALZ. On her advice, I contacted

Lynda Francis.

'As lesbians we were, of course, shocked when the President accused us of sodomy,' the fifty-year-old therapist chuckles. In her spare time, she counsels AIDS patients and gays who grapple with their sexual preference. She sighs deeply when I enquire about the 'ups and downs' of GALZ. She herself is white but says that it is becoming increasingly more difficult to associate with her own kind in the country. Running away, having oneself removed from the membership list and talk of emigration annoy her intensely. 'They saw GALZ as an association for get-togethers and parties and are now terrified to get politically involved,' she says, 'but what is the risk we are actually running? During the book fair there was a police car parked in front of the door. After I had offered coffee to the policemen, they slunk off.

'Of course blacks are also afraid, and they have far more reason to be, but a number of black members respond much more militantly to Mugabe's attacks. Perhaps because they are part of a tradition of resistance? Perhaps because they have got less to lose?'

Lynda Francis finds it particularly sad that the organisation is too scared to distribute a collection of experiences of black Zimbabwean gays and lesbians that was put together for the exhibition. 'But that makes it even more of a collector's item, a samizdat publication. Exciting,' she says while passing a copy on to me. 'Why don't you have a read, while I make tea?'

'I was lucky that I had a father who understood me. He knew of my relationship with Sipho,' I read in one of the contributions. 'One day I visited a cousin who taught me how to play chess. I got home very late. My father said that Sipho had come by and that he seemed to be very disappointed when he found out I was not there. Then my father told me that he realised that I was very fond of Sipho and that he knew we slept with each other. He was not angry with me. On the contrary, he said that it was normal in our society for boys to sleep together, up to a certain age. Young men were allowed to do so until they had served in the king's army. After that they were married off by their parents. Ndebele society is rather conservative. There are established rules on how to behave as a man or a woman at different ages. In any case, my father told me those things and said that he was convinced that it would come to an end one day. I was twenty-two at the time. I looked at him and thought that I would follow his example later. He never made me feel bad about my homosexuality, but he never encouraged me either. I think he left things open-ended and allowed me to be an individual.'

David, who grew up in the country, writes: 'When I fantasise about my future, I see myself living together with a friend in a hut, with some cattle and in a community that helps me to till the land. I see myself as a gogo, a grandmother. Although I cherish my dreams, I realise that the time is not ripe yet. Yet it is not impossible for I have already met a homosexual man who lived exactly like that in Matabeleland. I met him through an old school-friend. He is gay and has become a nyanga [traditional healer]. He wears traditional women's clothes, made of animal skin, and his house looks like a traditional African home. He is completely accepted by his community because he heals a lot of people. Homosexuality is often seen as an indication that a female spirit has taken possession of a male. If that spirit is helpful and encourages you to make yourself available to help the community, such a man sometimes becomes a medium. Especially if there is already another family member who is already a healer, as is the case with my friend. But if a devilish spirit has descended on you, who encourages a man to rape somebody, or whatever, you will be ostracised.' David told his grandmother that he was gay. 'She said that it must have been intended that way. There were already enough mouths to feed in the family.'

Shungu, in her turn, tells how she grew up in a rural area. She liked being with herd boys and hunting instead of doing her homework with the other girls. She was forced to marry a man. But that was a disaster and, after her divorce, she fell in love with a woman. The latter has since passed away, but Shungu hopes to meet a new partner one day.

Martha, finally, feels lucky because her beloved has promised her 'never to marry a man, only me'. She considers giving lobola, a dowry which usually takes the form of cattle, to her friend Ruth's parents.

When she comes back with the tea, Lynda Francis tells me that she emigrated in 1969 from England to what was then Rhodesia. After her marriage had failed, she realised that she was lesbian. In her new motherland, she plunged herself into the dazzling lesbian and gay lifestyle of the time. 'There were all sorts of gay bars in Harare, which was called Salisbury then, and you would bump into a considerable number of cabinet members,' according to Francis, who got involved in the course of the seventies in the resistance against the minority regime of Ian Smith. Independence in 1980, after years of gruesome civil war, was experienced by her as 'a rebirth' and since then she has felt Zimbabwean.

Independence hardly changed gay life. It was there, and everybody knew it, and at the same time the anti-gay laws, introduced in the nineteenth century by the allegedly gay British coloniser Cecil Rhodes, continued to exist. There was no talk of persecution, which according to Francis might have to do with the fact that Zimbabwe's first President, the minister Canaan Banana, himself preferred gay love. 'I remember going to a reception for the President with a friend in the early 1980s. My friend was dressed in traditional Ugandan fashion, in a dress, and all of a sudden felt the President's hand slide under his garment during the reception.' In order to qualify for the presidential soccer team, Francis says, 'one had to be very beautiful.' As a matter of interest, Zimbabwe had a law in those days that forbade citizens to make jokes about the President's surname.

However, it was only in 1989 that a gay interest group was established in Harare, and until July 1995 homosexuals lived a rather peaceful life, even if the number of gay bars was eventually reduced to one and this bar was not allowed to advertise itself as such in the media.

Perhaps the coming out of the gay movement, by applying for a stall at the book fair and producing its first publications, was one step too far and was interpreted as provocation by the authorities. Or perhaps, in view of the drought, economic malaise and the upcoming presidential elections in 1996, there was a political need for some sort of new scapegoat. Changes in South Africa might have caused nervousness in Harare's presidential mansion. It became clear that the 'freedom of sexual orientation' fought for by the gay movement was going to make it into the South African constitution, and the necessity for a genuine democracy and a presidential term of office that would not exceed two terms also seemed to have been agreed upon by the negotiating parties in South Africa. This was directly opposed to the beliefs of Robert Mugabe, who reluctantly had to give up his role as leader in southern Africa after 1990 to Nelson Mandela.

Meanwhile, Lynda Francis describes the President as a 'charming, intelligent, broad-minded person', with a remarkable memory. 'I met him in 1987 in my capacity as an AIDS worker. We spoke to each other for no more than five minutes. A year later I attended a session of Parliament and all of a sudden I came eye to eye with the President. I got such a fright that I dropped all my books. Mugabe made a beeline for me, picked my books off the floor and saluted me. "Good morning, Mrs Francis, how is your AIDS work coming along?" he asked.'

The therapist does not believe in the political explanations for the attacks on homosexuals as such. She can hardly imagine that Mugabe experiences the developments in South Africa as a threat. And, moreover, he should not feel concerned about the upcoming elections. No, Francis reduces Mugabe's attack to the personal state of mind of the President. 'I followed his speech on television and saw how he trembled when reading that passage. There was so much emotion in his tone of voice, it really came from the heart.' She suspects that Zimbabwe's President was sexually abused during his twelve-year-long incarceration under Smith's regime. 'It's common practice in our prisons. Moreover he was once branded as a queer by his white political opponents.'

Because there is no dialogue at all on the topic, many Zimbabweans also associate homosexuality with sexual abuse. 'If there is anything special about black culture, then it is its taboo on sexuality, any sexuality. I notice that in my practice. There are no Shona concepts for private parts or orgasm. And "sodomy" is hetero- as well as homosexual here. Women have themselves fucked "from behind" in order to avoid pregnancy. That is common. There is, however, a Shona word for gay: "ngochane". That means that our sexual preference is not alien to black culture.'

There is no witch-hunt shortly after Mugabe's speech, but there are incidents, frightening indications of what might follow. Lynda Francis gives an example. A couple of days before my arrival in Harare, the mother of a guy called Paul was phoned by a woman police officer. Was she was aware of the fact that her son, who goes under the name of a South African pop star, is gay? It could have hardly escaped her. Paul is a queen of the first order. The woman ordered the mother to send her son to the police station together with a thousand dollars. Paul consulted a lawyer on Francis's advice, went to the station and asked for the policewoman's official number. She refused to give it and all of a sudden had no time for the interrogation. She would be in touch with Paul.

According to Lynda Francis this incident demonstrates the dangers of blackmail, which Mugabe's speech seems to encourage. She has meanwhile laid a charge with the authorities and an investigation has been promised. 'But perhaps I am less scared of the police. They should, after all, keep to some rules. Homosexuality as such is not forbidden in Zimbabwe: you are only not allowed to practise it and therefore you have to be caught in the act before you can be arrested. I am more afraid of the ZANU-PF Youth Movement. If that is mobilised in the context of this campaign, there is no end in sight.'

What gays actually want is nothing more than to be able to do in private whatever other Zimbabweans do in that part of the house called the bedroom – undisturbed and unnoticed.

Peter, a law student, had been pondering for a while whether or not he should come out and tell his parents. 'After that speech, the whole family was talking about it. My mother said, "Leave them alone," but I know for sure that my family members will be less tolerant if I admit I'm gay.' So he decided to wait a while before he confesses. He is afraid of being thrown out of the house or of not being allowed to visit the pub. Peter finds it ridiculous that Mugabe praises family values and, in doing so, appeals to Holy Writ. 'What, for heaven's sake, is African about the Bible? It was introduced to this country by missionaries. My ancestors never gave me the slightest sign that I was not allowed to be homosexual.'

Errol, who sells flowers, does not understand the reproach that black homosexuals have copied whites. 'I have known for a long time before independence that I was like that. We lived in a township, far away from the white city. Even if I went there, the police would shove you off the pavement if a white person approached. Any contact was out of the question.'

'He wants to deport us, but to where?' asks Anthony in the maid's quarters in the evening. He hangs the two dresses that he has stitched together that day on a peg and asks in passing what I think of them.

'Great.'

'I am Zimbabwean: I belong here.'

February 1998. A land rich in metaphors. Plundered empty by a handful of erstwhile freedom fighters, like the Masvingo ruins. Hanging in the balance since, three years after Mugabe's gay-hate speech, the power blocks, which, loosely laid, represent a system of patronage and self-enrichment, are being levered out of position from all sides. Those who profit speak according to writer Chenjerai Hove in 'strange tongues' because they prepare their meals with the 'herb of forgetfulness'. His column in one of the few independent newspapers in the country, the *Zimbabwe Independent*, offers a weekly dose of antidote with which Zimbabweans hankering after change have their veins filled. A truth serum that is reminiscent of the ideals from way back, a struggle inspired by the desire to make a democracy of the old Rhodesia, stripped from its colonial rulers who had taken away the country for next to nothing from Matabele king Lobengula. The vana vevhu, the children of the earth, as the ZANU freedom fighters who recruited their members from the Shona majority in the country were called, fought a guerrilla war that caught people's imagination. This led eventually to the demise of Ian Smith's terror regime and to independence. When Robert Mugabe, a schoolteacher, came into power in 1980, neighbouring South Africa's hopes increased. Now it is the Zimbabwean gays who are inspired by

South Africa's sexual liberation.

The host who took me to a sidewalk pub shortly after my arrival in Harare is silent for a while when I ask him whether he has a partner. On the waves of revolutionary zest he moved to Zimbabwe in 1980 to assist with the demobilisation of 12 000 women who were part of the liberation armies. He fell in love with one of them. They married. The woman committed suicide two years ago. 'She was embittered,' he says, 'on account of the grabbing. That a corrupt bunch had come into being, that was only interested in self-improvement and forgot about the rest.' His tearful eyes betray a deep sorrow. Around us a mass of people sway to the rhythm of a West African band. 'It started with those women, who had also fought for their independence in the war. But after liberation this was not appreciated. They had to go back to the kitchen.' Their traumas, sustained on the battlefield and as a consequence of sexual abuse, were not important. Thereupon the modest funds for support of demobilised soldiers disappeared into the pockets of those in power and their pals. In its desire for majority rule the governing party ZANU thrashed the ZAPU opposition situated in Matabeleland in the early eighties. The bloodbath, which cost thousands of victims their lives, was described for the first time in mid-1997 in a report by a non-governmental commission of inquiry. The writers of the report make mention of their anxiety about reprisal. ZANU and ZAPU have amalgamated into ZANU-PF, but according to observers there is a time bomb ticking which can easily explode in future.

President Mugabe's tarnished image in terms of respect for human rights did not detract from his international reputation in the eighties. Western democracies failed to see the downward spiral of the economy, the muzzling of the opposition and media due to their focus on the neighbouring evil of apartheid. Similarly the International Monetary Fund showed a lot of patience in the soothing realisation that the economic malaise would eventually leave the Marxists-Leninists of ZANU-PF no other choice than the acceptance of a policy of privatisation, cutbacks on services and retrenchments in the government apparatus – in exchange for loans. The revolutionary rhetoric still lives on, but the 'strange tongues' combine a verbal hatred of the earlier colonial rulers with politics that have hardly brought about any changes to the existing power relations in Zimbabwe.

Mugabe's attacks on white farmers are no more than self-reproach. For Comrade Bob, as he is often referred to here, hardly did anything to arrive at a more just distribution of land or a stronger black grip on the economy. Only the new power elite profited shamelessly. Since over half of the Zimbabwean population lives below the breadline, inflation soars and staple foods have become too expensive for many, the authorities and state media are looking for scapegoats who can distract attention from their own failure. Recent victims include homosexuals, the trade union movement, which is blamed for behaving like a political party, student organisations, the farmers and the whites, who are considered to have a hand in every protest. A heavily patrolling police force opened fire on participants in a food riot in Harare in January 1998 on the President's orders. Eight people were killed. Members of the state security forces keep a continuous eye on executive members of the trade union federation ZCTU and were probably involved in the December 1997 attack on the life of their secretary-general Tsvangirai. Civil servants at the Ministry of Labour are preparing legislation leading to the dismantling of the federation while newspapers have been forbidden to give any attention to ZCTU's activities. In the draft legislation on the media sent to Parliament even 'checking of communication via e-mail' is announced.

Protest broke out towards the end of 1997 in unexpected quarters. Frustrations that had been pent up for years were released in a march of hundreds of war veterans. Some seventeen years after independence nothing had been achieved regarding the compensation promised for the years given to the liberation struggle. The President was scolded and besieged on the steps of his own party office. In that way the war veterans in a certain sense followed the example of the gay movement.

Having been cornered by the ex-combatants, behind whose protest Mugabe was unable to find any white orchestration this time, the government acted swiftly and efficiently. It was decided to give the war veterans a one-off grant of 50 000 Zimbabwean dollars and a monthly allowance of 2000 dollars. That smothered the protest. 'The cabinet has decided to make the war veterans part of its mafia,' in the words of a trade union activist. It worked for a while, but at the same time it engendered the rage of the trade unions and student organisations. Protesting against additional taxation used for financing the compensation, they had already managed to force the country to a complete standstill.

'Tomorrow we've got to do our shopping because on Tuesday there will be a stay-away,' Romeo says. He alternately crosses his arms one over the other, and then waves them around wildly. He is seated, his left foot bare and his right foot in a sandal, next to his friend Paul, who is wearing the left sandal. 'I wish he would just go away. Everybody is tired of him,' sighs the boy. There is audible approval from the others. The GALZ members are completely finished with Comrade Bob and form part of a slowly growing movement hankering after change. 'We were the first to dare contradict him. That had never been done before, but now everybody seems to be doing it,' Paul says happily.

To my not-so-small amazement I found the new, imposing

headquarters of the organisation in a leafy suburb of Harare. And it was black with activists. Three years after only a post-box number was left of GALZ, I find a movement that is in full blast. In the office people were busy with the production of a magazine, answering correspondence, the drafting of new proposals, for which foreign financial support is urgently required, the composition of a delegation to the 1998 Gay Games in Amsterdam and the preparation of a workshop on the role of the churches. At the end of 1998 the international assembly of the Council of Churches would take place in Zimbabwe. GALZ was setting all sails to get the gay issue on the agenda.

In a room behind the reception desk a black girl is bent over a lever-arch file. She looks like a little elf. Nyasha Mpungo is a theologian and assists the organisation with making contacts within the religious world. In Zimbabwe almost everybody is a member of a church. The pinpointing of allies within the different religious denominations is an important priority in the desire for equality. She is not lesbian herself, but had a lot of gay friends, explains Mpungo. They took her along to gay pageants, where she sometimes did the make-up for the participants. Now she helps out GALZ, 'like a nurse helps out her patients'. No, not that it is a disease, she hastens to add, shocked by the comparison that just escaped her lips. She considers homosexuality to be something 'entirely natural'. That black homosexuals would have allowed themselves to be tainted by whites, she finds ridiculous. 'Most whites have only found out of late that there is also homosexuality among blacks. They turned no one on.'

Nyasha Mpungo has lost a lot of her friends due to her work for GALZ. Within her family as well her engagement with gay concerns causes mixed feelings. 'My brother simply doesn't understand that somebody can be gay. My older sister is of the opinion that you either work for the Lord or for the devil. My brother-in-law cut all contacts. Only my younger sister doesn't have any problems with it.' And her uncle, who, after Mpungo's parents were murdered in 1981 as a consequence of faction fighting within ZANU, became a 'father figure' for her, asked when she told him of her activities: 'Are you now also going to become lesbian?'

Likewise the religious workers she contacts daily are very reserved. 'They only associate homosexuality with sex. They see gays as dirty old men, rapists, who can't wait for it to be dark, so that they can run around naked in the streets.'

But some are very curious and ask her to bring a gay person along to the next meeting they have. 'Show me one of them, they say. As if they have an idea that gays have an extra arm or one leg only.' Because of her work for GALZ the Baptist Church, of which she is a member, has suspended her right to preach. Mpungo hopes that the participating churches from abroad will help during the assembly to create a better understanding of homosexuality. That the Dutch Lutherans have meanwhile decided to boycott the meeting on account of Mugabe's repeated attacks on gays in his country doesn't really make sense to her. 'They should come and enter into a debate.' The Old Dutch reflex of immediately punishing reprehensible behaviour with a boycott probably played a part in this. Would it not be a stunt if the church nailed its homo-friendly doctrines on the front door of Mugabe's house during the assembly?

Within GALZ itself Mpungo's offer to support the organisation was initially not without controversy. 'Some women saw me as a threat because I also deal with men. In the beginning the rumour did the rounds that I was a government spy.' Similarly, the fact that her involvement is only recent was held against her. 'The situation with GALZ is similar to that of the government. For Mugabe you are a second-class citizen if you have not taken part in the guerrilla war against Ian Smith. In

GALZ people derive their status from the fact that they took part in the first protests after Mugabe had opened the attack on us.'

'Us?' she repeats in desperation. Then: 'Yes, us.'

❖❖❖

Tina Machida, twenty-eight years old and chairperson of GALZ for a number of years now, can also look back on a life of struggle. Against the school governing body. Against the church. Against the family. Against the police. Against her gay brother in the organisation. Against her white lesbian sisters outside. 'I knew it in boarding school already,' she says. 'I fell in love with a white girl. That was, of course, totally out of the question. I was of the same opinion, for I had more or less grown up in the church. God, did I feel sinful!'

Because Tina always played with boys at home, her parents were very worried. 'They thought I would turn into a prostitute later. They were thrilled when I brought a girlfriend home one day to stay over. But when my mother found us in the same bed the next morning she became hysterical and wanted to hit me. My father threw me out of the house that same day.'

Tina lived in the streets for a year. 'I slept close to the station. I was dead scared of men until I got to know Mike, although I refused for a long time to go to his home with him. I collapsed when he gave me five dollars and said: "If you don't trust me, you can immediately take a taxi back." I went with him and I discovered that he had established a shelter for street children in a shanty town. We lived there, fifteen of us, in one room. He told me that he himself had been thrown out of his home once and he saw this work as his mission.'

During the week the boys sold meat and cigarettes to stay alive. With what was left over, all the shelter kids went to a disco in town on a Saturday evening. 'There I was accosted by two men. They appeared to be policemen in civvies and they pushed me into their van. They took me home. I was locked up there and I was prohibited from continuing my studies which I had started. I was not allowed to go outside, only into the garden every so often. I was ... imprisoned.'

After a couple of weeks Tina's parents introduced her to a man. 'He took me to my room and he raped me. Day in, day out. After two months I was pregnant. In a certain sense that liberated me. Now I could do as I pleased. For having a child was exactly what my parents wanted. They thought I would get married sooner or later.'

Tina told Mike everything and then renewed contact with a friend whom she had got to know in the shelter and with whom she had fallen in love. 'She disagreed with my pregnancy. She thought that it had been conceived under the wrong circumstances and that I had to have the foetus aborted. After a few days we found somebody willing to do so. Secretly.' Tina was sick for three months, bleeding continuously.

Lighting up her umpteenth cigarette, she sighs: 'I do understand my parents. It is their culture. They are weighed down by the pressure of the rest of the family. There has to be a child, otherwise it is no good. And I actually don't mind having a child. I just don't want a husband.'

After her abortion Tina moved from one place to the next for fear that her parents might find her. Eventually she was phoned by one of her brothers with the urgent request to come home. 'There I was met by the entire extended family, and in Shona culture that means shut up and listen to what everybody has to say. You are not directly addressed, but are spoken about in the third person. Thus I was "told" that I was a whore and that I was no good, that they would change this and that I had to go to a traditional healer. "Can I also say something?" I asked timidly. "Shut up you," my uncle said.'

As in the case of Simon Nkoli, Tina Machida's family

dragged her from one nyanga to the next. The one burnt stones to steam out evil spirits, another prescribed medicinal herbs. A third pushed her in a dam to wash 'it' off. A fourth said, 'This is a guy,' after which her parents all of a sudden felt they needed a fifth opinion, but nothing helped. In their despair her family members placed all their hope in a 'Western' doctor, but he could not change her either. 'Then I ran away again and when they kept on sending my brother after me, I went back and told them that they should leave me alone.' For a long time it looked as if her parents had accepted the deviant behaviour of their daughter, until there was a photograph in the newspaper of demonstrators who taught Robert Mugaybe a lesson on their banners. Tina Machida was clearly visible in that picture. 'Then things started to get out of hand. They screamed over the telephone. They scolded me and threatened me. Initially I broke into a cold sweat, but I soon calmed down and made a plan.'

Slowly Tina sums up the decisions she made after much deliberation. 'First I thought: I will tell them that I had received a message from the ancestors. That is how you become a medium. And I'll tell them that message is from a deceased aunt or from a niece. In any case from a woman, for if that is the case, Shona culture allows one to marry a woman. But when I thought about it again, I rejected the idea, as I did not want to be a nyanga at all.'

Tina then decided to initiate a relationship with a friend of hers. 'He is a very good friend and he knows that I am lesbian. This is very handy as it brought some rest to the family and, moreover, if you want to rent a room here, it helps if you are a heterosexual couple. So when I was looking for a place to stay again, he came with me and we pretended to be a couple. He might also become the father of my child, because when I thought about it, I realised I very much wanted to have a child.

But before this can happen, I first have to have myself tested and find out whether everything, on account of the abortion, is in order now. And furthermore I want to make sure first that he won't demand the child at a later stage.'

Tina's most important defence mechanism is situated in the very creative way she deals with culture. 'In Shona culture grandparents have a larger say over the first-born grandchild than the parents do. My grandparents are of the opinion that I should get a child, but they don't think it is necessary for me to marry first. I suspect this has to do with a deceased aunt of mine. She stayed unmarried her entire life. I think she was lesbian and that my grandparents are not as shocked by my homosexuality as my parents are. As long as they live, I am safe, but when they die, I have a problem.'

'Do you know, Sarudzai,' – already within a couple of hours I have been given a nickname in the GALZ office (flattering, but not very applicable: gift) – 'you sometimes get very tired. The struggle never stops and if it is not directed against your family, then it is against the boys in GALZ, for in the end they are ordinary men and therefore look down on you. You are good enough to listen to their love problems, but when it comes to executive positions, they don't think you are suited for that. It has taken a long time to break that way of thinking and eventually, by the grace of God, they allowed me to become chairperson. No, in the end I only feel at home with women, with black lesbian women specifically. I don't feel at all at ease with white lesbians. They have their own forum, the Women's Culture Club, and only invite you when a donor comes by. That looks good, a black butch in the audience.'

Keith Goddard was one of the few whites who stayed faithful to GALZ in those dark days in 1995. 'After the book fair Lynda Francis and I convened a meeting and asked the black GALZ members: "Please, take over. It is the only way of guaranteeing that GALZ remains a militant organisation in future."' The new black executive members, in turn, asked Goddard not to abandon them. Today the thin, hunched man is one of the two paid secretaries of the organisation. Goddard was also given a nickname in the office: 'Lekker Ding'. His name can be found throughout the improvised archive, which is put together in some lever-arch files: minutes of previous meetings, newspapers, pamphlets, invitations for parties. There is also a letter from a young man who alleges that the GALZ secretary seduced him. The seduction is not what the letter-writer objects to; rather, that since he lives in poverty, the time has come for compensation. The young man demands several thousand dollars and provides a budget detailing how he will spend the money: new shoes, new clothes, a CD player, food and so on. If necessary, Goddard can send the money in installments. If he fails to oblige, the young man threatens to take further steps. 'It doesn't affect me,' Goddard says softly, 'but it is a typical example of something that happens regularly here. Meanwhile GALZ could use the assistance of at least three lawyers. The minute we hear of a new blackmail attempt, we get into action. This also influences the police's behaviour. The more cases, the more policemen know that they have to keep quiet.' Goddard is not surprised by the systematic extortion practices in his country.

The scandal in which ex-President Banana got involved is a case in point. The minister who, after Mugabe took over from him in 1987, lectured in theology at the University of Harare was accused in July 1997 of having sexually abused several of his employees. The attack was opened by Jefta Dube, a former bodyguard, who was on trial for murder of a fellow officer. That crime, as Dube confessed, was the result of an uncontrollable anger he felt rise in him when his colleague alluded to the sexual relationship Dube had with the President in the early eighties. 'My colleague and I were taking a leak. He started to taunt me, to badger me. He called me Miss Banana. I totally lost control of my senses,' Dube stated in court. He was apparently forced into a relationship by the President and was regularly forcibly intoxicated. 'Then I woke up and my body would be covered with sperm.' After Dube, several other ex-colleagues came forward with identical accusations directed at Canaan Banana. The ex-President, married and father of three children, rejected them out of hand. This was nonsense, he was after all a theologian.

GALZ could not entirely suppress a certain enthusiasm in its first reaction. Banana seemed to be the living proof of the nonsensicality of Mugabe's statement that homosexuality is 'un-African'. It manoeuvered the President into a very uncomfortable position, even more so because almost everyone assumes that he must have known of Banana's sexual escapades. Nowhere in southern Africa is there such a well-organised secret service as in Zimbabwe and, moreover, 'everybody in Harare knew about it,' according to Goddard.

Very soon, however, it became apparent that the affair would also feed into the popular belief that homosexuals are rapists. 'We quickly let go of the idea to offer Banana our support,' according to another GALZ activist. 'If he had just admitted his sexual preference and had joined our organisation, then we could have talked about it, but his denials actually seem to uphold that culture of secrecy.'

Shortly after Dube's accusations the ex-President was indicted. The hearing, for which several churches have already made financial support available, has been postponed several times. In April 1998 the court in Harare announced that Banana's counsel had requested the case be dismissed and that the request had been turned down. Keith Goddard expects that the affair will eventually be swept under the carpet.

Meanwhile the police seem to be increasingly aware that the continued hysterical attacks by Mugabe are no longer a licence for blackmail or badgering. The administration of justice in the country is still independent enough, at least for the time being. Goddard says: 'Sometimes I have the feeling that I am being followed. It also seems as if they are tapping my phone. From time to time there is a patrol car in front of the door of the GALZ office and pictures are taken of visitors. During our last AGM we decided to demand prints. Aren't we entitled to that?'

'Do you know,' says Romeo, who is known in the office as Rosie, 'this is actually also exciting – our struggle. In South Africa all anti-sodomy laws have been abolished and there is even talk of gay marriages. Good, but then it also becomes a bit boring,' he says while pushing his right sandal onto Paul's foot. Paul adds: 'It is also nearing the point where you think: fuck you, I couldn't be bothered anymore. Yesterday one of our members left for a conference in America. We waved goodbye with flags and GALZ banners. "Where is your white lover?" a cleaner asked curtly. Then I introduced him to Romeo. Look, this is my friend, I said. He is black and I am not dependent on him. You should have seen the look!'

Yet so far it doesn't look like the fuck-you mentality of the GALZ members will ever point the country into the direction of neighbouring South Africa. And it is not the tangible resistance of continued protest that will in the long run make the Zimbabwean President shudder. No, it is the thunderbolts and gale-force winds, an ancestral warning and a passionate affair that will make his flesh creep. Thus in the beginning of 1998 lightning almost struck one of Mugabe's holiday homes and a gust of wind landed a tree on the porch of his official residence. Heavy weather almost crashed the plane in which Mugabe was travelling to Mozambique. These are signs, meaningful signs on the basis of which traditional healers tell him that he should change his style of governance or should leave altogether. They appeal to a contact with Mbuya Nehanda, who was executed by a British firing squad in 1896 after she had led a revolt against the settlers. And then there is the affair of the cleaner, a family member, who made love on the king-size presidential bed, in yet another holiday home, with a bodyguard. When that was exposed, Robert Mugabe decided on a deed that wipes out memory. He had the bed burned.

It was the same old song. Exactly a year after Robert Mugabe's outburst, the President of Namibia, Sam Nujoma, also felt compelled to lash out against the homosexuals in his country. A Western aberration, un-African, sickly ... Nujoma had taken good note of his neighbour's words and used a congress of SWAPO's Women's League as his audience. This time there was no gay movement's request to register a stall for a book fair – there was no movement at all – but two transvestites got things going. In a toilet in the hotel where the League had convened, they had touched up their mascara and straightened their suspenders. That went down the wrong way with one of the representatives, so she complained. The President would teach them ... Many participants, however, were surprised at Nujoma's unexpected outburst. What was it that he meant by 'degenerate homosexuals'? They did no harm to anyone, did they?

Presumably the editors of *Sister Namibia*, a magazine with many lesbian contributors, would have ignored Nujoma's remarks – considered it just dumb rhetoric – if an overzealous press officer of the governing party had not gone ahead and said it all again. 'That really was the limit,' says Liz Frank. 'Whoever we called within SWAPO, nobody knew what the spokesperson based his opinion on nor whether Nujoma represented the party's policy with his remarks. There had never been any discussion.'

The women of *Sister Namibia* took the initiative and held a public meeting. Ian Swartz was one of over one hundred who attended. 'We could not stomach the fact that Nujoma had made those remarks nor rather could we believe that he could have made them. After all he is some sort of father figure, the first President of independent Namibia. Many moffies said, "He does not mean that: he just read out a speech written by somebody else. He always does that." But the subsequent press release could not be taken lying down.' During the meeting, the Rainbow Project was established. Just like in Zimbabwe, the authorities achieved the opposite of what they had aimed for: gay activism came out of the closet and accelerated into a higher gear. But unlike in Zimbabwe there were discussions on television and in the printed media.

In an open letter to the SWAPO press officers, printed in *The Namibian* of 31 January 1997, Niko Kisting, one of the newly elected executive members of the Rainbow Project, wrote: 'Enough is enough. You accuse "Europeans" of infecting us with sickly aberrations such as homosexuality. But many of those Europeans supported the struggle against the occupation of our country by South Africa. Several gay movements collected money for SWAPO and took good care of our exiles.' Kisting recalls how he was abused because he refused to conscript into the South African army. In the late 1980s, he fled Namibia with the intention of joining the SWAPO army in exile and undergoing military training. 'I kept silent about my sexual preference for fear of being abused again.' When he heard from compatriots in Zimbabwe that a real witch-hunt had begun for alleged spies in the military camps of the freedom movement, of which hundreds of SWAPO fighters had become victims, he backtracked and settled down in a European country. He finished his studies and, after independence, returned to Namibia in 1989. 'Meanwhile,' he wrote, 'this moffie feels man enough to stand up for his rights. But what about SWAPO? Does the movement feel man enough to finally face up to the atrocities which its members committed in the military camps? In order to admit that almost ten years since independence, nothing has been achieved with regard to a more honest distribution of land?' Kisting saw the attack on homosexuals as an attempt to draw attention away from Nujoma's own shortcomings.

Following Nujoma's remarks Elizabeth Khaxas also felt compelled to go public about her sexuality. 'I have always lived a little bit on the edge,' she wrote in *Sister Namibia*. 'My parents did not understand why I wanted to study as a young girl. My fellow scholars did not understand why I wanted to continue my education instead of going on strike against apartheid. They called me a "white foot", a traitor. In my country, as a black person, I was considered to be inferior and I had taught myself not to see myself as a "=nu khob", a black skin, but as a "=nu khoes", a black person. As a woman and a single mother, after all, I lived in a world that is physically, economically and sexually controlled by men. Now I am free. Although these days I now worry that parents from the school where I am the principal will want to get rid of me when they hear I am a lesbian. The law does indeed forbid this, but can I be sure that the officials of the Ministry of Education will support me when push comes to shove?'

Nujoma and his party did not appear to be men enough during the weeks of the debate to answer the many questions that were thrown at them. But, unlike in Zimbabwe, the critics actually made an impact.

The secretary-general of SWAPO's Women's League, Erica Ramakhutla, made it known that she could not find any clause in the constitution that prohibited homosexuality. That the law made sodomy (anal sex between men) punishable seemed wrongful to her. After all, wasn't it also practised by certain heterosexuals? Prime Minister Hage Geingob went out of his way to dampen the fire after foreign donors threatened to withdraw their financial support to Namibia. 'Nobody has ever been convicted in this country for homosexuality,' he said, 'and I do not see any reason to change that.'

With hindsight, the Rainbow Project team offers a variety of different explanations for Sam Nujoma's unexpected outburst. Ian Swartz: 'He always parrots Mugabe. This does not only hold for the gay theme, but also for the land problem. Mugabe attacks white farmers, Nujoma attacks white farmers. Big words with precious little action.' His friend, Steve Scholtz: 'I don't have the impression that he has experienced something that made him build up distaste for gays. He does not really seem to be interested in the subject. Nujoma is moreover not a big intellectual. He utters something and when someone responds, he does not know what to say anymore.' Liz Frank: 'He does not want to be seen as Mandela's lapdog. So, once in a while, he thinks of some way of making it clear that we do things differently here. That South Africa has gone so far in such a short period of time as far as homosexuality is concerned, is seen as proof of the fact that Mandela may appear to be in charge down south but the whites still have the final say in South Africa.'

Moreover, according to these three people, the fact that SWAPO, in contrast to its Zimbabwean sister party ZANU-PF, backed down so quickly is largely due to the difference in age between the two decolonised nations. Liz Frank: 'Independent Namibia is ten years younger than Zimbabwe. Rot has not set in here yet. There is still some sort of spirit. Unlike ZANU-PF, SWAPO has not alienated itself from its grass roots. Many Rainbow members sympathise, incidentally, with SWAPO.'

Namibia is a village where everybody knows everybody in the

political arena. That also helped when the Rainbow people began their offensive. And then, of course, there is the rumour that a son of one of the highest politicians is 'also like that'. It also happens, even in Namibia, in the very best circles.

Now that the dust created by the short anti-homosexual explosion has settled on the sand of the Kalahari Desert, the young Rainbow Project is racking its brains over what it should do next. The homophobes within SWAPO, once a seasoned guerrilla movement, have strategically withdrawn. And it is difficult to fire on a target that has gone into hiding.

▽▽▽

Holiday resort Zum Potjie and hotel Zum Sperrgebiet. A window of a photo shop, full of prints of the latest Damenabend (ladies' night) with its inevitable climax of three boys in dresses: bizarre. Just having finished a Brötchen Leberkäse (liver sandwich), I am accosted by a black doorstep salesperson who offers the *Allgemeine Zeitung* with an entrancing smile. Likewise, a black woman behind the desk of my friendly hotel says 'Bitte?' when I ask for the keys to my room. Later that evening, three members of a Prussian elite corps suddenly march into the Biergarten of the hotel. The executive of the local carnival association, so I am told.

My hotel, Thüringer Hof, is situated on Independence Avenue, Windhoek's main road and one of the few indications that the country has recently gained independence. There is a strange atmosphere in this town, which sits at just eighteen metres above sea level, its 150 000 inhabitants existing at a dry place between the Namib and the Kalahari, the two oldest deserts in the world, in a country that is twenty times the size of The Netherlands. They call it Africa here but it feels like Germany.

What am I to make of the Cohen Gebou (building) just round the corner from the Goering Strasse, diagonally across from my hotel? Isn't Goering the father of ... ? But who was Cohen?

The many Konditoreien (coffee shops) and Bierstuben (beer halls), the Königsberger Klopse and the Thüringer Bratwurst leave such a mark on this city that you could believe yourself to be playing a part in one of those famous German detective series. With 'Schwarzen' (blacks) who make a nuisance of themselves by walking in front of the TV.

I have so many questions to pose to the mayor, presumably a veteran freedom fighter who can show with fantastic sleight of argument that there is indeed an African town hidden somewhere behind this strange illusion. But Doktor B. Graf Finck von Finckenstein is abroad, visiting family in Germany, the mayor's secretary tells me the next morning. And yes, of course he is a SWAPO member.

I am standing in the centre of Windhoek, in front of the monument to the 'brave German soldiers who helped in the struggle against the rebellious Hereros and Hottentots (1903–1907)'. A soldier on a horse, a tribute to men who butchered some 55 000 Hereros, an ancient nomadic people. Another 5000 were chased across the border into Bechuanaland (now Botswana). Less than a third of them were left at the end of it all. That is how the German colonisers, for whom the Berlin Conference in 1880 earmarked Namibia (and Cameroon and Tanganyika), responded to the rebellion of these oppressed people – people who, on account of a rinderpest epidemic which nearly wiped out their cattle, were forced to seek employment with German families – and suffer the consequences. The rapes, the beatings and the murders which their employers inflicted on them brought their anger to the boiling point. It was Lieutenant-General Lothar von Trotha who gave the orders by signing a Vernichtungsbefehl (extermination order).

Later in history, Chancellor Helmut Kohl refused to meet with the Herero paramount chief on his official visit in 1995, but President Roman Herzog was more respectful in March 1998. After a conversation with the chief, Herzog called this carnage 'a black page in our bilateral relationship'. Herzog was of the opinion that the campaign could not be justified in any way and 'was a weight' on the already heavily laden conscience of 'any German with a sense of history'. But Wiedergutmachung (restitution) was out of the question. 'In those days, there was no international rule of law to protect rebels and civilians,' it was said. What seemed to worry Herzog more, as became obvious the next day, was the language policy of Namibia's government. After independence, German was no longer one of the official languages of the country, and therefore it is in danger of being marginalised, according to the President.

The conscience of the approximately 5000 Germans in the Namibian diaspora does not seem to be burdened by any sense of guilt. Grand monuments keep the memory of shameless lynching parties alive, without their being so much as a note saying 'Nie wieder' (never again).

But the South African settlers have also left their mark. In the museum next to the brave German warrior, a wall plaque recounts the fate of King Mandume. Back in the nineteenth century, the chief of the Ovambos, who are the largest population group in Namibia, fought the South African farmers, who, in turn, had come to the rescue of a group of Portuguese farmers in Angola who had no respect for borders and were trespassing on Ovambo land. During an attack they wounded Mandume and he kept his honour by putting a bullet through his own head. That Mandume's head was subsequently chopped off and, as a horrifying example, exhibited in the centre of Windhoek is entered only as a footnote to this tale.

Nobody seems to be bothered by this. There does not seem to be anybody who in the dead of night wants to pour a big pot of red paint on the head of the brave German soldier. Similarly nobody seems to frown at seeing the Nazi memorabilia in an antique shop in Swakopmund. On the contrary, they even seem to attract a specific type of tourist to this resort, where literally everything is German.

Perhaps it is only a bewildered stranger like me who finds all of this a little bit suspicious, but even that feeling seems to dissipate after a while. Leopold Klaassen, a Dutch surgeon whom I meet one evening in the local hospital, tells me that during the last carnival parade in Swakopmund, there were again men who raised their right hand and called 'Sieg Heil'.

'But that does not mean anything,' he says. 'It is the same as "Oranje boven" [a resistance slogan used in The Netherlands during the German occupation].' Massacres, witch-hunts for alleged spies, the Holocaust … amnesia has hit Namibia hard.

What on earth could have moved the President to accuse homosexuals of behaving in an un-African manner in a country where a haze of Gewürztraminer constantly cloaks and hides anything truly indigenous?

Just like the welfare worker who after a number of years sees fraud in anyone on the dole, Leopold Klaassen has lost all faith in Africa. 'All they do is kill each other,' says the surgeon, who at one time reported for duty in a South African homeland with a backpack full of idealistic intentions to do good. Even if the Namibian nurses aren't as lazy and fat as their southern neighbours, he has had enough. In autumn he will return to The Netherlands for good, cured of any belief in progress. 'I'm only keeping criminals alive,' he states.

With his Swedish colleague Chris Priwe, a dentist appointed to the same hospital because he was the only one prepared to treat AIDS patients, Klaassen shares the desire to have a good, long conversation after hours during the long and lonely night, which comes to an end with the assessment that he arrived at long ago: that things will never succeed. Not in Namibia, not in Africa, not with blacks, not with gays. He sneers at the possibility that you might lose yourself in a romance once in a while. 'They are given to drink, are involved in prostitution and are polygamous.' Moreover, he already has a partner. In America. No, he'd rather read a good book.

But Chris cannot stop himself. Bald and in his fifties, he has launched himself into a new affair again, even though he knows 'that you are always being used and that all everybody wants is to see money.' Moreover, it will never last: 'because, in the end, you won't take any illiterates back to Europe with you.'

His young black friend Robert, a student at the University of Windhoek, listens in silence and apparently approves. It is an embarrassing ritual whereby the white men both stress that their generalisations do not, of course, apply to Robert. He is different. Chris knows how to make something out of nothing with this young Damara, one of the many population groups in Namibia's ethnic ratatouille. They see each other every evening, except for Wednesdays when Chris goes to ballroom dancing in a hall full of swastikas. A welcome distraction from daily worries.

❦❦❦

It was the drags who were the first to stick their necks out. 'They were never bothered by what people thought: they always paraded proudly through the township. With an attitude of "I couldn't care less". And when the drag queen pageant took place, *le tout* Windhoek would show up; but now this is no longer appreciated, not even by the gay movement,' says Sonia Maffeis, a half-Namibian, half-Italian documentary film-maker. She got involved in *Sister Namibia* five years ago.

'There was a gay organisation then, the Gays and Lesbians of Namibia (GLON), but it was entirely dominated by white males. There was nothing in it for me, and eventually the organisation evaporated. But butches found a home in *Sister*.'

Together with her Afrikaans partner, she joined the Rainbow Project last year. 'We feel more at home there than at GLON.' But in a certain sense the organisation still has not managed to escape Namibian reality. 'Within Rainbow everybody withdraws into his or her own circle. At parties one immediately turns to one's own kind. Butches with butches. Whites with whites. Coloureds with coloureds. Basters with Basters. Activists with activists. Middle class with middle class. That's the way things go,' she says with a sigh.

Moreover, the gay movement has not yet managed to make contact with like-minded people in the black townships situated far out of town. 'But we have discovered a gay-friendly shebeen in Katutura, run by a lesbian and her father. Perhaps that is a starting point.' But the gay movement is not entirely free of racism. 'Some time ago a German lesbian said to me: "You're doing a good job – the only drawback is your being non-white."'

The film-maker is collaborating with Steve Scholtz on a strategic plan for Rainbow, her partner being the treasurer. She has a clear vision of the future of the organisation. 'We need an office and we have to put together a set of rules and regulations. Meanwhile efforts have been made to set up a parental support group. We have to attract attention by encouraging public debate: then we'll be on our way to Katutura.' There seems to be a need to raise 'issues' with which the group will get publicity and exposure. 'We have recently had to deal with an issue concerning a resident permit for one of our members. Liz Frank is of German birth and she was refused a permit. But when she approached a lawyer and initiated legal proceedings, the judge decided that her lesbian relationship with Elizabeth Khaxas entitled her to such a permit. A big victory. We were very excited.'

Another issue that is high on Rainbow's priority list is the recruitment of allies. 'We are now supported by the Legal Assistance Centre, the Ombudswoman, the Anglican church and the Windhoek Schlachterei [butcher].'

Excuse me?

'Yes, they sponsored our posters.'

She worked out that she was lesbian at a young age. 'My mother secretly hopes it will pass. She is on her own now and is proud to have a strong, independent daughter, but her daughter's lesbianism seems to be one step too far for her,' she says laughing, 'and it does not want to go away.'

Her German stepfather was not pleased at all. 'But I did not have anything to do with him really. He was an asshole, who nailed a picture of Adolf Hitler next to my photo in the bedroom. What else can I say?'

Maffeis's partner's parents are still unaware of their daughter's sexual preference, even if she has been involved with *Sister* for over ten years now and is living together with Sonia. The bank where she works – they know. 'They think it is okay,' she says softly.

Maffeis is working on a documentary, which she hopes will be screened by Namibian television. 'It is called "Beyond Identity" and I want to tackle everything in it: racism, tribalism, xenophobia and homophobia. This country tends strongly towards the conservative and in response to that the government squashes everything that is deviant from the norm. This is no solution. People have to learn how to overcome bigotry by talking about it, not by covering it up. Only then we can grow towards something better.'

'When we established Rainbow, the German butches immediately came out with their own brochure. This was lavishly illustrated with dildoes, entirely S&M. I did not mind ... it had style,' says Sonia, 'but if you remark on it, they have it in for you. Then you would take away their right to their own culture, but they forget that their opinions and values exclude people like me.

'We can learn to live with the pamphlets. More frightening is what happens at parties. There they walk around in their corduroys, and if you don't hide you might be forced to dance sakkie sakkie to Afrikaner concertina music. Women hold each other tightly around the waist and press their pelvises together, with their shoulders alternately going up and down.' Her face says it all. 'But in the course of the evening it becomes really dangerous,' her friend continues. 'Then they get drunk and throw each other onto the pool table. Some men are too scared to come.'

has the Truth Commission called you yet?'

The old, stately army corporal smiles a little, shrugs his shoulders and then says: 'You don't let up, do you?'

'No, I'm serious,' Dawie persists. 'Don't you follow the stories of what has really been going on?'

'When P.W. Botha came to power, I retired. It was only after that that everything went wrong,' his father, Patrick, says irritably.

'Ag man, you know better than that. Steve Biko tortured to death. The children of Soweto shot. Neil Aggett thrown out of a window. That all happened before the Groot Krokodil came to power.' His son flings the accusations at his father's feet.

'I was involved in supplies. I cannot be held responsible for anything. And no, they did not call me. What would they want from me anyway?'

I have not even introduced myself and Dawie has already dropped a bombshell. 'My parents have always supported the National Party, have always defended apartheid,' he tells me on our way to Hoedspruit, close to the border with the Kruger National Park. 'Now they are old and I don't think they can change. But I am filled with anger and I cannot stop myself from showing it.'

Dawie stands in the middle of his parents' lounge, gesticulating wildly. 'They dished out Mandrax in the townships; that's how they tried to get the children on drugs, so that they kept quiet. They spread AIDS: they made men with HIV sleep with black whores. Men with HIV on a mission! Didn't you read about it?'

His father is silent, his mother on the couch stares straight ahead. She tries to calm her shaking left hand with her right hand.

'It is just as well that you have Alzheimer's,' says Dawie, when he tries to break the icy silence with a joke. 'Then you don't remember your Parkinson's any more.'

A house full of secrets. A father who does not want to divulge anything of his military experiences, of which his son thinks the worst. A mother who cannot divulge anything any more. Her racist reflexes only come to the surface once in a while. When the two black kids that Dawie has just picked up from the township – he is some sort of foster parent – enter the living room, hold out a hand and say 'Dag Ouma' (hello grandma), she snaps: 'I'm not your granny.'

'All right Ouma,' says Patrick.

And then there is Dawie's homosexuality which, hidden for many years behind an apparently happy married life, has now come to full fruition after his divorce. It is not only this different lifestyle that goes against everything his parents have believed in all their lives, it is also that he discovered he liked black men, and very young ones at that. How do you go about explaining this to people who cherish their whiteness and imagine themselves to be part of a chosen people? 'I can't,' Dawie said this morning on our way to Hoedspruit.

When he has finished his long tirade against the atrocities of the apartheid period, we sit down at the table and enjoy our meal. His mother desperately tries to transport the pieces of pork chop from her plate to her mouth. When she has finally finished eating, she is exhausted and wants to go to bed.

'What is happening to them?' she asks getting up slowly, referring to the two boys who are indulging in hamburgers and French fries in another room.

'They'll stay here for the night,' Dawie says. The shaking little woman turns even paler than she already is. One can read the anxiety in her eyes.

'I'm only joking,' says Dawie.

Put at ease, she shuffles to the bedroom, supported by her husband.

The clock strikes nine. 'Come on guys,' says Dawie, 'I'm going to take you home.'

Quickly he puts a twenty-rand note in each of their pockets. This is followed by warnings. 'Don't spend it on drink. Do your homework. Especially your English: that's the most important subject. If there is a problem, ask Oupa (granddad). He will tell me.' The boys nod politely in acknowledgement and jump into the car.

When they are gone, the old man opens a bottle of wine. 'Dawie is a free spirit,' he says. 'He is a law unto himself. He has always managed but sometimes I wonder how he will cope when we are no longer around. His catering firm is not doing well. Themba [Dawie's partner] did a moonlight bunk. A couple of months ago, he was given notice because they are going to build a hotel on the site of his house. But perhaps Kaffir will find new employment in Johannesburg.'

Kaffir?

'That's what I've called him all his life,' says the father. 'Why? No idea. Perhaps because he behaves like a black man.'

Dawie's nickname often caused confusion in this white hot town in the Northern Transvaal.

'Once I was looking for him and asked in the bar of a hotel whether they had seen my Kaffir. The owner said: there are no blacks in this bar.' His father roars with laughter.

'Dad, I'm very worried,' says Dawie when he comes back into the house. 'Mum goes downhill every day and you keep on pretending everything is under control, but I can see you are dead tired. She has to be taken to a nursing home. Why don't you accept that? Don't keep on playing the old army corporal.'

'Ek sal sien [I'll see].'

When we get up, he asks whether Dawie has heard anything from Themba.

'Nothing,' he says. 'I think he's in Ermelo, with his family. We'll drop in there tomorrow.'

'You and Themba are partners,' his father responds. 'You belong together. I pray that he will come back to you.'

'What does he mean by that?' asks Dawie as we leave.

It is already late in the evening when we drive off to meet Gert. During his infrequent visits to Hoedspruit Dawie always visits his old school-friend. 'Then we start drinking, man. And we talk about life. You can have fantastic philosophical conversations with Gert,' Dawie calls out excitedly as we pick our way along the zigzag forest path on the way to Gert's house. After a while we can see lights flickering in the distance and, a little later, we stop in the middle of nowhere, enveloped in nature.

Gert has built his own shelter from the world at the border of the Kruger Park. It is full moon. The men embrace.

'Watch where you put your feet,' says Gert. 'The elephants made quite a mess here last night. I think they were curious, but I slept through it all. Didn't hear a thing.'

He unscrews a bottle of brandy and fills our glasses.

For a full minute of 'silence' only the sounds of the night are audible. The shrill sound of the crickets, a scream once in a while, a sigh, a shriek. A hyena, a leopard, an elephant. Gert confidently recognises each and every sound.

'How are you keeping in Johannesburg?' Gert asks.

'I'm having the time of my life,' Dawie says. He pours himself another glass. 'Skyline, Club 58: man, that's enjoying life.'

Gert himself went to Club Zoo the other day. 'Nature is great, but sometimes it gets to you, and you need to escape. So I travelled to Johannesburg on the off chance. Somebody had told me about the club ... in Yeoville, jeans, leather, a West African barkeeper in a tanga. This all appealed to me but at the door I was told to take off my pants. It was "pants down evening". "Hang on, I left something in the car," I yelled and off I went. Skyline is just as cosy.'

We laugh.

'I'm a volunteer with the gay movement organisation,' Dawie continues. 'We are currently organising a film festival and in two months' time it's Pink Saturday.'

'A gay parade,' sighs Gert. 'That's what we should have in Hoedspruit.'

'Yes,' says Dawie, 'the two of us. Marching with a banner down Voortrekkerstraat ... Can you imagine that?'

Another glass.

'Out with it,' says Gert when we stop laughing. 'Themba?'

There is a long silence.

Gert fetches a new bottle of brandy and fills the glasses.

'Perhaps I should let go of him,' Dawie says. 'Some time ago João from Maputo was here. I felt we could have started our relationship again, just like that, but I hesitated, had to think of Themba all the time.' Dawie gets the hiccups and chokes on a gulp. When he stops coughing, he continues with a thick tongue. 'I can't go on without him.' Then, sobbing out: 'Just tonight even my father said we belong together.'

Gert puts an arm around Dawie and strokes his back. 'Bedtime,' he says.

The next day – in this environment lorded over by elephants, giraffes and leopards – I, a mere human, am sick as a dog. The brandy has temporarily made life a touch fragile.

❦❦❦

I met Dawie six months ago. It was a Sunday evening and he was looking for a mutual friend, who had stayed in my house for a while. Stephen, however, was not at home, and I did not know when he was coming back. Dawie, who could have walked straight out of a French cheese commercial or, alternatively, could just as easily have passed as Middle Eastern, introduced me to a short young black man who shyly walked behind him. His name was Themba, he was eighteen years of age, and he was Dawie's 'companion'.

'Every weekend we drive to Johannesburg. Monday morning we buy vegetables and meat at the market. In the afternoon we drive back to Hoedspruit and deliver to hotels and restaurants,' Dawie explained.

The three of us watched a documentary on the Truth and Reconciliation Commission. In fact, Dawie only listened … to the heart-rending testimonies, which followed rapidly one after the other. For an hour he hid his face in his hands, sighing deeply every other minute. There was the story of the woman who wanted to have the hacked-off hand of her murdered husband returned to her. This had been preserved in formalin, she had been told, as a trophy at the local police station. There was the request of a thin young man in a wheelchair who wanted a bursary to study as compensation for the fact that the police had shot at him for no reason.

When the programme on the TRC was over, Dawie's tear-stained face reappeared and he said: 'We did not know it. But why didn't we know, when others did?'

Dawie's emotions confused me. Touched by the fact that he did not hide behind his upbringing, church, television and education, I felt moved to comfort him: 'Hey, it wasn't so bad.'

But it was bad. After two years of the Truth Commission, those who knew, know that it was worse than we ever imagined.

'How can we still live knowing all this?' Dawie wondered.

That's how perpetrators are turned into victims.

Perhaps he wanted to free himself of the burden of the past by seeing Themba as an equal. They are not only lovers, Dawie rather quickly confides in me (although Themba looks embarrassedly the other way when the topic is raised), they are also 'business partners'. The 'company' – nothing more than a bakkie stuffed with food that travels up and down the freeway – belongs to both of them. Eventually Dawie would like to hand over the whole show to Themba.

Their presence in the house on Sunday evenings became something of a habit after that first time and, after a while, they also stay over. That's how I gradually get to know two Thembas: the real one – a shy young man who does not let anybody in on his deeper thoughts: just once he mentions that he'd rather sing than sell vegetables – and the Themba as Dawie likes to see him. 'He is very introverted, but once he's relaxed, we have very good discussions,' says Dawie. 'Themba knows exactly what he wants. Still waters run deep. But Themba is going to turn our company into a world-class business! He sees me as his best friend. Just last night he assured me so again.'

So Dawie was over the moon ... three days before Themba disappeared for the first time. Now, every so often there is a sobbing man on the phone, who all of a sudden pops in at my house because he has an appointment with a psychiatrist in Johannesburg. Who wandered through Hillbrow in the evenings, because that's where Themba would be hiding out, and who desperately phoned all over the place to get some idea of where, perhaps, he might be ... Who would eventually find

Themba again, somewhere in a squat, after which they had long 'discussions' in the bakkie, and sometimes at my place, where I found out that these were not discussions at all, but a monologue by Dawie, just as would happen later in that lounge in Hoedspruit, in front of his father, and that Themba would respond as little as the old man does. He only nodded once in a while and usually agreed to return with Dawie to the Northern Transvaal.

Then there would be another honeymoon period and the company from which many customers had withdrawn their business would flourish once more. Until Themba disappeared again. After which the search started all over and this desperate man was likely to crumple to the floor in my front hall because his blood pressure was too high. After a minute he would get up again, would make some phone calls, or schedule another appointment with yet another psychiatrist who would confirm that the depressions, which were now occurring quite regularly, had no psychological cause at all. Now he had pills and, sure enough, 'I've just taken one and I feel much better already.' All that remained was to find Themba.

He found him, that last time, somewhere near a petrol station where he washed cars. Just like six years ago, when Dawie met him there.

'Please join us,' Dawie asked, when he had brought Themba inside for the umpteenth 'discussion' in my flat.

'But it's between the two of you. Themba will only feel intimidated,' I objected.

'He appreciates your opinion ... please.'

In my bedroom the quiet young man sat on the edge of my bed.

'Themba wants to break off our relationship,' Dawie said. 'He plays in a band and has spent all his savings making a CD which isn't selling. I am not surprised. Those record company guys are no good: you can see so straight away. Why didn't you tell me, then I could have got myself involved!'

Themba taps his forefinger on his left leg, bored.

'Break off the relationship ... Do you know what that means?' Dawie continued. 'What are your chances of achieving something?'

A Gordian knot of feelings – a mixture of guilt and sexual desire – is suddenly hijacked by an intrinsic dominance.

A sobering moment. Was Themba too stupid to see that – without a home, without a company, without any prospects – he could learn so much from this man?

Themba got up and walked out of the bedroom. 'It does not make any sense,' Dawie said bluntly and then collapsed onto the bed. And there he remained for a good couple of hours.

❦❦❦

'Do you really think this the right thing to be doing?' I ask when we are on our way again, this time south from Hoedspruit towards Ermelo.

'A girlfriend, marriage, a child ... I know that Themba does not really want this.' Dawie appears to want to save the boy from a heterosexual delusion, despite believing 'our relationship won't work out anyway: I have given up hope on that.'

'Really?' In answer, Dawie simply turns up the car radio.

'I know for sure that he is in Ermelo. I have not been able to find him anywhere in Johannesburg: I looked in all the likely places. He's probably taking responsibility again for all the problems in his family. His damned stepfather an alcoholic, a mother who passively accepts whatever happens. And Themba just keeps washing cars so that there's food on the table.

'He must get out of there.' Again a secondary motive seems to justify this mission.

'But if he wants contact, then surely he could have phoned you?' I try.

No response.

Shortly before Ermelo, the township of Wesselton appears on the horizon.

'What were the directions again? First head in the direction of the township and then take the left turn-off,' Dawie says. We approach the built-up area and decrease our speed. Dawie braces himself, and takes a deep breath.

'Is this sensible?' he mumbles. 'Is this sensible?'

We have almost reached the turn-off when Dawie suddenly swerves to the right and continues on up the highway to Johannesburg.

What did he think about it? It didn't matter. If his colleagues in Zimbabwe and Namibia felt the urge to attack homosexuals, that was their affair. They might have their reasons for doing so; he didn't. After all, Botswana didn't have this problem anyway. And so Sir Ketumile 'Quett' Masire was silent on the matter. He had other things to worry about.

In a sense, the silence of Botswana's President, who has since been succeeded by Festus Mogae, is regrettable. Because, of course, the 'problem' does exist. Perhaps a vitriolic verbal volley would have propelled the gays of Gaborone out of their hiding places for good, much as it has in neighbouring countries.

'I can easily make do without the small luxury of holding another guy's hand,' young lawyer Mpho says during a meal in the restaurant of the President Hotel in Gaborone. It is one of those hidden gay places, as is the Gaborone Hotel (or GH, standing for 'Gay Heaven' in popular gay parlance). You'd have to be blind not to notice Mpho is gay. Rings on every finger, a silk scarf around his neck, his one leg elegantly crossed over the other, and camply dangling a cigarette, he looks like a black Quentin Crisp. But his friends, he says, 'have learned not to ask awkward questions'. So nobody knows what everybody knows.

Of all of them, only Patrick has dared to come out publicly. It came about when, in an attempt to initiate discussion a couple of years ago, the Human Rights Centre, Ditshwanelo, invited speakers who were pro- and anti-gay to an open debate; but the gay young men who came along left early. They did not feel they needed to listen to a church minister's discriminatory ranting and apparently they did not feel up to responding to him.

Only Patrick stayed on, asking for permission to speak later that evening. 'We are not dogs nor pigs. We are not un-African. We are your blood,' was one of the things he said. The local newspaper reported Patrick's speech the next day, pretty much verbatim, and they mentioned him by name.

'I was afraid that my family would read it and would speak to me about it. The journalist had not asked for my permission at all.'

The family, however, kept quiet – equally ready to keep mum and not ask any awkward questions. Ironically his gay friends turned away from him, decided to ignore him in the streets and in the hotel bars. They no longer wanted to be associated with him.

Alice Mogwe, the director of Ditshwanelo, sighs deeply when she thinks back to that meeting. She would love to dedicate herself to the liberalisation of the homophobic legislation in her country and would like to be actively involved in the setting up of a movement. But how can her centre give priority to this if gays themselves pretend not to exist?

There has been an attempt to set up a gay support group, but the name Ditshwanelo in itself reveals the reluctance of the people involved to organise themselves on the basis of their sexual orientation. The group would implicitly support gays, rather than explicitly fight for their rights. Encouraged by the tempestuous growth of the movement in South Africa, and long before Robert Mugabe's attacks, there was, at one point, a short period of planning meetings and brainstorming sessions. GLOW chairperson Simon Nkoli was even invited to run a workshop.

'But it didn't lead to anything,' says Mike, who had a relationship with Simon at the time, and who wanted more than anything to follow his example. He lacks, however, Simon's charisma, his gift of the gab and his conviction that things will come right as long as you keep going, all of which characterised his then lover. The man with the beard and the friendly eyes appears shy and constantly throws the conviction of his words into doubt by grinning self-effacingly.

'When I visited Simon in Johannesburg, I was constantly inspired by the enthusiasm of the GLOW meetings. I was not afraid to kiss Simon in public on Pink Saturday. And that was even shown on television here. Then I would go home with great ideas and plans, but the closer I got to Gaborone, the further my courage sank out of sight. In the end, hardly anybody came to our meetings any more,' he says, a little embarrassed about such seeming incompetence. 'Here in Botswana, we were pretty well handed our independence on a silver platter back in 1966. We never fought for it. It is not our custom to fight for anything here.'

And it is extremely hot.

Still, Mike thinks there is scope for a group to be formed.

'When at the time we sought publicity for our initiative, we were overwhelmed with letters. I recall somebody writing: "I am the only gay in Botswana, but I have slept with over a hundred men."'

'Botswana is not as it appears,' says Marijke Overeem, a Dutch woman who stayed on after being involved in ANC activities in the eighties. She found a job in education, and became fond of the country.

'At the time, people wanted to know why I had dedicated myself so much to the ANC. So much sacrifice, was that worth it? But I was flattered to be asked! The Spanish civil war had passed me by, as had the resistance in the Second World War. When people travelled en masse to Nicaragua to defend the revolution, I was at university. Finally, I was able to make my contribution here. And now I live here. What else could a person want?'

She is fascinated by Botswana and the way in which, after the diamond discoveries in the 1970s, it transformed itself from one of the poorest countries in the world into one of the fastest-growing economies in Africa. A multi-party democracy without any foreign debt, where human rights seem to be respected. A well-organised health-care system, a reasonable level of education. No corruption. A success story to which World Bank reports often refer.

'But that is not how things really are,' says Marijke decisively when we are on our way to the psychiatric clinic close to her school to visit a friend. 'This country is like this clinic. It looks clean, and on the surface the atmosphere is pleasant, with nurses dedicating themselves affectionately to the care of their patients; but we don't see the people who are knocked out with sedatives, who are unnecessarily punished and nagged – and we don't see the wards that patients are never allowed to leave. There is abuse of power and a hidden cruelty.'

She continues: 'The health-care system is reasonably organised, but forty per cent of the population is HIV-positive. We have the highest stats in Africa.'

This is due, in part, to the high mobility of the Batswana and the San who, in the early days, worked as migrant labourers or lived the itinerant life of herd boys in the veld. Now people find employment in the cities, many hours' distance from their home village. It often happens that men employed by the government are put to work in the north, and their wives, often teachers, in the south. And then there are the single mothers, sometimes with children from different fathers, men passing through who feel no obligations at all. But hardly anyone talks about these things. AIDS prevention campaigns barely get off the ground and the government refuses to make condoms available in prisons. Because, of course, no sex goes on there – or so it is said.

'And of course there is corruption,' says Marijke. 'Why would things here be different from the rest of Africa? It is not unusual that a Minister calls a company here and orders something. When it is asked where the invoice should be sent to, the Minister will ask: "What do you mean, the invoice?"

'Oh sure, there is a Parliament and there are different parties, but out in the country the tribal chiefs have the final say. Botswana is still semi-feudal and heavily based on a system of patronage. Consequently, your position in the governing party or opposition is closely linked to where you are from and your tribal grass-roots support.'

That the local economy is growing cannot be denied. 'But for whom? In the cities there is an emerging middle class and there's lots going on. But the minute you take a side street, poverty stares you in the face.'

Meanwhile it is time for lunch and Anastasia has joined us at the local coffee shop. She works as a secretary for one of the highest judges in the land. After my presence has been explained, homosexuality comes under discussion.

'Due to the talk shows on South African TV, which we can receive here, I now know there are also black gays,' she says in desperation. She really couldn't care less.

Whatever the foreign visitor wants is his affair; but what she really wants is for someone to make the issue go away.

'Once I was approached by a lesbian woman. She made advances and then I ran away.' The country's high rape statistics are, in her view, due to 'frustrated gays who cannot get any herd boy they want and therefore have to prove that they are a man.'

On our way home, Marijke comments: 'At puberty boys were sent out into the bushveld, far away from the community. It was not unusual to have sex at the cattle post.'

Just as it sometimes happened that boys had their first sexual experience with a Western missionary or a teacher from abroad.

'That's what happened to two men I know quite well. A foreign teacher, that was exciting. A rock music LP was put on, you were given a cigarette and a glass of wine. After which there was some fondling. And it was all over with. In the process, you probably also gained some sense of freedom. For a moment you could withdraw from the traditional social system, from the strict norms applied by society. You could, for instance, say much more to an older 'friend' of that sort than you ever could to the elders in your village.'

It sounds dangerously like sexual abuse on a grand scale – and real grist to Mugabe's homophobic mill, confirming his statement that Westerners are responsible for the promotion of homosexuality in Africa. Marijke shrugs her shoulders.

'I don't have the impression that anyone was traumatised by such goings-on. It happened, and it was exciting.'

And, in many people's estimations, it did not amount to homosexuality per se.

'It was something that went unnamed. That is not unusual here. Westerners always want to stick a label on everything. We want to know exactly what somebody died of. Not so here.'

A culture of secrecy has developed in which much more is possible than in the West. The division between heterosexuality and homosexuality is therefore less sharply drawn. Or so it might appear …

▽▽▽

Marijke's words haunt me as I listen to the stories of Mike, Mpho, Patrick, Joe and Lester in the bar of 'GH'.

'By the time I was eight, I already knew that I was gay,' says Patrick. 'It was exciting to touch somebody's prick. When I was eighteen, I left for Gaborone and there I heard about Mpho. I found his number in the telephone directory and we made an appointment. He ... initiated me. If I still had doubts, they disappeared there and then. It was great.'

Now Patrick's mother also lives in the capital. 'She thinks it is quite normal for me to take a male friend home once in a while. She makes my bed and prepares a meal. My male friend and I sleep together, but my mother doesn't ask any questions. In the morning she brings tea. Our culture is very hospitable.'

But why was Patrick so afraid when his name was mentioned in the newspaper? He chooses not to reply.

Joe also has an understanding mother. An elderly woman, she lives in a village not far from Gaborone. 'When I told her that I am gay she told me that she had always considered me a girl.'

'Can I visit her?' I ask.

Joe is suddenly terrified: 'Oh no, that is impossible.'

Mpho says it is 'terribly easy' to hook up with someone in a pub. 'You watch each other, you smile a little, you drink a little and then you go home with him. When you get there, you say "Let's romance" and then you have sex. But after three days, you will find out that he sleeps with girlfriends when you are at work. Then you leave again, but this does not stop me from trying again.' Things just did not turn out the way they appeared to be.

Mike's coming out initially led to tensions in his family.

'I already knew when I was seven, but I chose to forget. When I had a girlfriend years later, my memory returned. Shortly after that, I got involved with a South African exile and told my brother, who in turn told my parents. They were furious but after a while we managed to talk about it. And because this secret had come out, all of a sudden other things were being discussed. I, for instance, wondered how it was possible that my brother had such a big bum. That only happens if you have Bushman blood. My father had always said we were Basarwa, but when I mentioned it, he conceded he was of Khoi origin.' Just like in Namibia, the original inhabitants of the land, the Khoi-San, or Bushmen, had become outcasts without any rights. So it was better not to look like them.

Lester, finally, outdoes all the others when he asserts that he knew he was gay when he was only five. The hairdresser enjoyed prancing around in his mother's dresses and putting on make-up.

'My grandmother had no problem at all with my homosexuality, but she thought I should get married and have children. My brother would have to help me with that.'

❦❦❦

Many stories do the rounds in this silent country. Like the one about the beautiful herd boy that Mpho tells me the next day.

'I saw him and was immediately besotted with him. I introduced myself, he introduced himself. We talked about this and that, and then I told him I found him very attractive. I asked him whether he wanted to sleep with me. He was not shocked and just said: "Sorry, but that is not my culture." When I told my friends, they all laughed at me. "You should not have mentioned it," they shrieked. "You should have just done it!"'

Alice Mogwe remembers another tale about two lesbians in Gaborone. 'At a certain point, everybody knew. And so the rumour started that a couple of lesbians had arrived among us. Even the lesbians in question heard the story and thought: Great, two more. And for several weeks, they also started looking for these two new lesbians!'

'Inter-racial relationships are quite normal here,' says the priest, who is originally from New Zealand. Eight years ago, at about age forty-five, he was posted to Gaborone. His activities as assistant to the Archbishop are augmented by his journalistic work for a radio station.

It had struck me before that Alice Mogwe is married to a white Dutchman – and in the streets of Gaborone, the visitor will regularly come across mixed couples. This is not South Africa. 'I don't quite know why this is so,' says the priest, 'but no one bats an eyelid at mixed couples here.'

His nineteen-year-old friend Philip, a civil servant, softly strokes the palm of his hand every so often. They have been lovers for several months now. The young man spends the weekend with the priest, after which the latter takes him to work on Monday morning. 'When my colleagues ask me who this white man is, I always tell them he's my brother-in-law. Nobody seems to mind.'

Initially I feel a bit uncomfortable about this hypocrisy, but in the course of the conversation, my attitude changes totally. A man of his age? Why doesn't this young man look for another friend? But Philip is too scared to come out to his family and finds the priest's house a safe haven over the weekend. After five girlfriends, he is now completely convinced he is gay. When he spends time with the priest, he can listen to his wise stories, often recounted with a sense of humour and dry understatement; and he gets to meet like-minded people such as Mike and Joe.

A thought comes to me: yet again a missionary uses a religious 'alibi' to make himself comfortable. But the priest says: 'The church has had a devastating influence in Africa. Missionaries have always sharply condemned homosexuality, but have also been most active in "spreading the word".'

In the past, a Ugandan lover had tried to blackmail him. The priest takes up the tale: 'He made an appointment with the Archbishop and told him I was gay. If he were given money, he would keep his mouth shut. The Archbishop sent him away. In the evening the Archbishop asked me: "Why did you not tell me. How can I defend you if I don't know what you really are?"'

❧❧❧

The museum at Serowe is as silent as a grave. The town, two hours' drive from Gaborone, is the birthplace of Seretse Khama, the first President of independent Botswana. It is a public holiday but the caretaker is prepared to open up the exhibition space to me for a while.

The rooms are full of photos from the fifties and sixties. They show a stately man in beautiful Western suits, always accompanied by a trim white woman in a two-piece suit. It is Lady Ruth Khama, a British woman whom the tribal chief had fallen in love with while studying in England. This got him into serious trouble. 'What are you up to with this white woman?' his tribal elders asked him when he came to introduce her.

A meeting was called. The men of Serowe listened resignedly to Seretse's story. First there were a number of questions, but when it came to the vote on the relationship he was given their blessing. The tribal elders raised some objections and banned Khama and his wife to a remote village, presumably under the influence of the South African government, which saw the presence of a mixed couple in the Presidential Palace just around the corner as quite abhorrent. But eventually Seretse Khama's choice was accepted and he was inaugurated as President.

His son Ian has since become Vice-President.

❧❧❧

The hotel in Serowe, on top of the hill, seems to be a symbol of a faded glory. There are no guests. It is already late at night when I sit myself down at the long bar. The hotel manager pours a glass of wine for me. Just down from the bar there is a dark passage with a couple of chairs in front of a television mounted high on the wall. I can see a young man in the corner watching an American B-movie. For a moment, we glance at each other. After a few minutes, our eyes meet again. He smiles faintly and I can see a row of glistening white teeth. Dark pupils framed fiercely in white. The game is repeated time and again. He pretends to watch television but those pupils constantly move in my direction.

Is this what it seems to be? Does he fancy me? Should I start a conversation, tell him I'm interested in him? Or will he tell me with a smile that that is not part of his culture? We look and look.

As I walk away I feel his eyes drilling into me.

†here is, of course, a French anthropologist. Africa is full of French anthropologists. Her name is Nicolette, she has wavy blond hair and she studies the cultural monuments of the Basotho people. Comfortably ensconced in the reading room of the museum in Morija, she sits bowed over a pile of documents, making notes. Her pen moves busily across the paper as if the research requires great haste. When I sit down opposite her, she smiles. Adolphe Mabille, however, looks sternly down at us: the somewhat faded photograph on the wall shows the old missionary complete with long beard and a dark suit.

There is, of course, an American historian. Africa is likewise the continent of American historians. He knows everything about Lesotho's history. At the end of the 1960s, he left his country and the Vietnam war behind. In the meantime he has become a full citizen, a white Basotho. A friendly man, he shows me his modest domain, which smells heavily of the past. Dinosaur footprints; volumes of the *Leselinyana la Lesotho* (the 'little light'), the oldest newspaper in sub-Saharan Africa; a family tree of the royal family, Moshoeshoes and Letsies. In the library he leafs affectionately through old missionaries' diaries, having blown the dust off. Then he pulls out a file and says: 'There must be something. I know for sure that something has been written about this, and not so negatively either.' He works his way quietly through the pile of magazines. He's got all the time in the world.

And then there is Kefuoe, the stable boy, who dropped me off here after a pony trek through the mountains. When I look outside through the window, I see him smoking dagga on the porch of the museum. He inhales slowly with his eyes closed. Suddenly he gets up and blows the smoke into one of his horse's nostrils.

'Then she'll be quiet tonight,' he told me earlier.

I am not quite sure what I am looking for here. But what I find is an impressive history of a people whose origins lie in two initial waves of refugees and 'reformed cannibals', as the tourist brochure teaches. Those were the years of *lifaqane*, the big drought, of war and the formation of the nation. Of the rise of Shaka Zulu in Natal, who chased away hundreds of chiefs to the area of the Basotho. These are the years of colonisation by the Boers, who chased the original inhabitants of South Africa, the Khoi-San, coloureds and mountain people in the same direction. These were the refugees; but nobody knows where the 'reformed cannibals' came from …

The beginning sounds like a fairy tale. The nation was brought into being by Chief Letlama. He was taught by Chief Mohlomi to take care of the poor, to be generous to friend and foe, to be peace-loving, to work hard, never to kill anybody who was suspected of witchcraft and to marry many women. In that way he would be able to extend his influence among the many clans in the land. This polygamous principle served the purpose of building up a united nation, which Letlama (later rebaptised as Moshoeshoe I) would rule for almost forty years.

More than one hundred years later – Moshoeshoe died in 1870 – the history of Lesotho is buried in a number of rooms in the museum of Morija, a village south of the capital Maseru. The village's name is derived from the biblical temple Mount

Moria (God's care), where God supplied a lamb to Abraham to sacrifice instead of his son Isaac. In the 1830s, the missionaries of the evangelical society in Paris settled in Morija. They had arrived here to relieve these primitive people of their superstitions and convert them to Christianity. Away with witch doctors, polygamy, initiation rituals and lobola! Those upright men with beards, like Adolphe Mabille, were initially quite convinced of the superiority of Western civilisation.

As it happens, almost all Basotho have since converted to Christianity; but their traditional beliefs live on as well. The missionaries had no other choice but to accept this.

'We have', Adolphe Mabille said in an attempt to improve the troubled relationship with some of the chiefs, 'perhaps learned more from the Basotho than they from us.' After which he – and many years later, his British successors (Lesotho became an English protectorate in 1868) – dedicated himself to the development of education, helped establish a newspaper and encouraged talented Basotho to write prose and poetry in their own language.

It would therefore be unfair to blame the missionaries, or even the British colonisers, for the fact that there is very little left of Moshoeshoe's ideals. In 1966, what had been Basutholand became independent under King Moshoeshoe II. Since then, tens of thousands of Basotho have migrated to work in South African mines, resulting in over half of the national income of the poor kingdom being accounted for by migrant labour. Likewise many of the educated middle class, which is pretty large in Lesotho because of the educational system set up by the missionaries, move immediately after graduation to South Africa, which draws job seekers like a magnet with its equity and affirmative action policies in both the public and private employment sectors.

After a number of palace revolutions and military coups

democracy was re-established in Lesotho in 1994, but in February 1996 the officers at police headquarters in Maseru mutinied following accusations of corruption. The land suffers from erosion, urbanisation is too rapid and there is a definite drain of adults. The agricultural methods are outdated and women are still considered to be second-class citizens. Does the country still have a right to exist?

'Perhaps, in the end, there will be more monuments than people here,' anthropologist Nicolette says bitterly, collecting her things together to leave.

A country deserted by its own people.

Outside Kefuoe says: 'I love Lesotho, but the only thing I can do is guide a visitor through the mountains. I finished my schooling, but there is no work. Can I stay here? If there is a big fish swimming out there and I can catch him, I'm leaving.'

Silently we drive into the village.

All of a sudden he asks me: 'Are you married?'

I shake my head.

'Do you have a girlfriend?'

Again I shake my head.

'But you have to ... How can you do without?'

'Oh, there are other options,' I say.

Of course, how could he have forgotten.

'Fine with me,' he smiles.

Almost everything in Morija is historic. During our trip, Kefuoe and I pass the old church; the cemeteries; the oldest house that somehow escaped destruction during the First Boer War in 1858; the *Leselinyana* printing house; the (once) mission schools; and Jubilee Boulevard, an avenue planted with oaks in 1908 to celebrate the arrival of the missionaries seventy-five years before.

Having toured the village, we reach the king's palace, Thaba-Bosiu, after an hour-long trek through the mountains. Below us, in the valley, lies Maseru. 'King Moshoeshoe II,' explains Kefuoe, rolling his umpteenth joint, 'returned from exile in 1994 and was reinaugurated.'

The winds of change, as I understand it from his words, had also blown from South Africa into Lesotho. In March 1993, the Basotho National Party, which had only survived thanks to many years of support from the apartheid regime, traditional chiefs, the Catholic Church and some West German sponsors, lost the elections. The Basotho Congress Party (BCP), which sympathises with the ANC, gained an overwhelming majority. But the army resisted the BCP's rise to power: their allegiance was to the National Party.

In April 1994 the newly elected vice-premier was murdered and in August of that year King Letsie III, appointed by the military, suspended the constitution and proposed a transitional government. 'The Basotho responded with a massive stay-away,' Kefuoe recalls. 'Moreover, South Africa, Botswana and Zimbabwe came to our rescue.' The result was that King Moshoeshoe II returned from exile and ascended the throne.

'There still has not been any investigation into what really happened,' Kefuoe says.

Meanwhile the house in the mountains is again inhabited by Letsie III.

'Our royal family has become tarnished,' Kefuoe feels.

'The nice thing was,' the guide continues explaining the rich past of his country on the way back, 'that the Basotho developed a pride for the values taught by Mohlomi without any attempt at a narrow definition of ethnicity.' It is presumably on the basis of that definition that the Basotho offered refuge during the apartheid years to many South African activists on the run. 'The apartheid government, however, saw us as a model of their homeland policies,' he continues.

But Lesotho is no longer a place of refuge. Zulu kings no

longer chase chiefs away, nor are there reformed cannibals. The South African activists have gone home and the mountain people hide out in Cape Town. Of the Basotho people, only the very young and the elderly stay behind, clad in blankets. We stable the horses and say goodbye. Tomorrow is just another day.

❦❦❦

He has found it, after ploughing through lever-arch files and boxes. The issue of *Shushu* has surfaced. The archivist hands it to me with some pride. Mugabe's and Nujoma's homophobic outbursts were of little interest to the authorities in Lesotho, but a civil servant in the Ministry of Information had at one stage seized the opportunity to publish a letter to the editor in an official information brochure. Next to the letter is a photograph of the author. The young man describes how in 1995 a gay bar was opened in Moshoeshoe II, a suburb of Maseru. This was all right until passers-by started to make rude homophobic remarks. Then the pub was closed. The letter writer does not understand why. Why did people meddle?

Thus, the beginning of a public debate was at the same time the end of it. The fact that the letter was printed in an official government publication seemed to indicate that the official point of view was that gays should not be harassed. 'That's what we would like to believe,' says the archivist hesitatingly.

But where does one find gays in Lesotho? He does not know.

❦❦❦

Three months later. At the border post near Maseru, it looks as if I'm entering the country against a huge wave of emigrants. A combination of factors has brought me back: the desire for a peaceful drive through the mountains; Kefuoe's wisdom; the sight of a distraught professor in an empty room; the mysticism of the French anthropologist and the house on the hill where I fancy myself a king for R60 a night. In his office in the museum, the archivist leafs through a memorandum of a working group which suggests making Lesotho the tenth province of South Africa. He sighs as he reads through the document. Then the telephone rings and, in the course of the conversation, I hear my name mentioned. When he puts down the phone, he says: 'That was Kefuoe. He has been working in Johannesburg for a month now and he sends his regards.'

Kefuoe has apparently caught that big fish.

Skyline's fate has echoed Hillbrow's, the suburb in which the pub is situated: it has changed colour completely over the last ten years or so. The process started at the beginning of the 1980s. While the rest of the country applied the Group Areas Act to the letter, the Hillbrow authorities turned a blind eye. For security's sake, new black inhabitants registered themselves under white names, but nobody made an issue of it. Hillbrow had always been different.

Henk Botha, who established South Africa's first gay magazine, *Exit*, in 1983, remembers the arrival of the new inhabitants quite clearly. 'Initially there were no problems. People were moaning, but they always did when there were new groups of immigrants. It had not been any different with the Greeks and the Italians, but in the end everybody was always accepted in Hillbrow. And people are not as obsessed here by the colour of your skin as in the rest of the country.'

But Hillbrow's tolerance imperceptibly cracked under the influence of an influx far greater than that of the European fortune hunters who had first populated the area.

Right up to the 1990s, it was the club district for a large number of whites, but now there are very few who actually want to live there. That the integration of black and white in the suburb was so smooth was, according to some people, due to the fact that there were so many gays living in Hillbrow in the early 1980s. However, the outcome of the then exclusively white elections of 1987 raised some doubts about the exemplary behaviour of so-called progressive whites. The election was won by Leon de Beer, a National Party candidate, who had presented himself during his campaign as a fighter for equal rights for gays and as an opponent of integration. He did not think the black influx was problematic, as long as there weren't too many. There are very few white moffies left in Hillbrow.

These days the suburb is almost completely black, beyond integration.

It is eight years since I first visited this bar and I still like going there on a Saturday evening. But in May 1998 I am part of a diminishing white minority that does not allow their fear to take over in a South Africa that is addicted to fear. Nothing has ever happened to me in Hillbrow, but when friends point out the crime statistics to me there is very little I can say.

Of course, I notice the sirens of the police vans that regularly shriek past and I have stopped telling people that things are not as bad as they seem. I suppose that the possibility of a modest adaptation of this passage in a future print run should not be excluded. But, for the moment, I do not feel unsafe.

On the contrary. On this fresh autumn evening in May 1998, Skyline feels like that warm bed which I felt myself falling into on that very first visit. It is full: the room sweats. To reach the bar I first have to wade my way through a bevy of hugs. Looks of recognition. There are no doubts about my order: my vodka with ice is already waiting for me at the bar. The contents of the jukebox have not changed in years. The absence of whites is richly compensated for by the presence of lesbians. From the day of Mandela's inauguration as President, Skyline has also been open to women. Because I got to know so many people and have kept in touch with their lives, I have perhaps gained a sharper insight into the world behind this pub. At present a visit to Skyline makes me feel sad, but also slightly envious of South Africans' capacity to leave their cares behind them and get completely involved in the happiness of the moment. 'One Night in Heaven'.

❦❦❦

Jozef has taken me to meet his grandmother. The evening before he had participated in the Miss Skyline contest and he had created quite a stir with his second-hand dress, third-hand wig and provocative stance. But he failed to win and that was a pity because taking top prize could have been the beginning of a modest career as a drag queen. Last year's winner has subsequently become very successful in both the northern suburbs and Soweto.

As I had been accompanied by a photographer for a magazine story, Jozef had introduced himself and offered to be the subject of our story. Perhaps he felt he would get access to eternal fame – and hence income. He knew all the drags in the township and there would be no problem introducing them to me. A visit to his grandmother's house, where he lived, could also be arranged. But what he really wanted was to be photographed.

So we were on our way to Soweto. He tells me he already knew he was into boys when he was ten. This was on account of a teacher who asked him to pull down his pants and then touched his buttocks. 'I enjoyed it, but other people, of course, think that it was forced upon me this way. Nonsense. That teacher made me aware of what was inside me.' Just like when his love for women's clothing was awoken initially by a videotape of Evita Bezuidenhout, the enormously popular TV and stage personality created by the now-famous Pieter Dirk Uys. 'Also family,' says Jozef. 'Family' means homosexual in gay slang. A 'Priscilla' is a police officer, a 'Lettie' a lesbian.

Then Jozef's neighbour introduced him to dozens of other

drag queens in the township. 'I knew some of them. I had seen them parading in the streets, waving at taxi drivers. Everybody seemed to enjoy that, those screeching queens with fake bosoms. It was all a big spectacle.'

But here reality beats fiction too. 'On the surface nobody seems to be bothered, but if you start joining in and you dress up at home in front of the mirror, you will get different reactions,' says Jozef as we drive into Soweto, and that is all he wants to say about it.

'Are you sure your grandmother won't object to us taking pictures of you in her house?' I ask.

'No, really ... it won't be a problem ...'

We park in front of the modest house and knock on the door.

'You're lucky your uncle isn't here,' the grandmother says bluntly to her grandson when we explain the reason for our visit. 'One day he will murder you and it will be your own fault.'

Jozef sits with his head bowed on the bench and keeps his mouth shut.

'His uncles say: if you really do have to be gay and prance around in a dress, why don't you make money out of it?' she continues. 'But I think he's a man and that he should behave like a man. This is not right. I pray that he will change.' For a moment she looks up at the portrait of the Pope above the wall unit and crosses herself. After which she says: 'When he was seven, he became very confused. That I understood. Shortly before my daughter had been murdered by Jozef's father. My grandson had some psychiatric treatment and for a while things went much better. Now he is confused again and he wants to walk around in dresses, but this time I don't see any reason for this silly behaviour. All that make-up: what a waste. My heart can't stand it,' his grandmother wails despairingly.

Jozef says nothing and inspects his feet.

We decide to leave and have the photo session at my flat.

'He is too old to understand,' says Jozef, who becomes much more talkative about his grandmother on the way back to town. His use of language is characterised by careless gender references.

'What is that lump in your neck?' I ask him when he suddenly happens to turn around.

'My uncle.'

'That cut on your forehead…?'

'My uncle.'

'You're missing two front teeth.'

'My uncle.'

This uncle, as we swiftly learn, has developed the habit of banging on Jozef's bedroom door, kicking it open and beating the young man up.

'But he won't beat it out of me. I'm doing what I want to anyway,' he says with a grim face. 'I know what I am.'

'Are you in a relationship?' I ask.

'My lover died last year in a car accident.'

I switch on the car radio. There is an announcement on the news that Mandela has met with two representatives of the gay movement that afternoon. 'Equality is for everybody,' the President said on the stoep of his official residence. 'The time that the state interfered in the private lives of its citizens is long past.'

'Good,' said Jozef. 'She is right.'

At home, in the bathroom, he puts on the shabby dress from the evening before. It's the only garment he has, handed down by a neighbour. He puts on pantyhose under his slip and then the wig. The hair just covers the scar near his temple. He puts mascara on his eyelashes and powders his cheeks. Then he steps into a pair of well-worn pumps. He runs into the room and hums along to 'I Will Survive'. Jozef is radiant and starts to chat up the boy from next door. That was more like the Jozef we knew.

❦❦❦

Tonight at Skyline Jozef is dancing the night away. When he spots me at the bar, he leaves the dance floor and wades through the crowd. 'I've got nothing to complain about,' he says when I ask him how things are going. Meanwhile, he has moved in with a friend, in whose hair salon he earns some extra money, and his uncles have stopped bothering him. 'It became intolerable in that house,' he says. 'Last year I was on television, in a talk show on homosexuality. When I got home, they really beat me up. I had put the family to shame, and they would knock it out of me. The next morning I staggered to the railway line and lay down on the track. But there was no train and after half an hour I thought: I'm not giving them that pleasure. Then I moved in with Richard.'

Now he is happy, all the more so because the white man across the bar – Jozef nods in his direction – has had a note passed to him. A name and a telephone number. 'I won't ring him, I'm not that stupid. But it is good to know that I am still desirable in the marketplace.'

The man on the other side huffs at me after Jozef has walked away. Then he recognises me and waves, mostly in order to attract the attention of the two young black men on his left. They are much more interested in each other. When he falls against one of them 'by accident', he is pushed aside in a friendly manner.

Barry, a man in his fifties, has been a regular at the bar since the time it was called The Butterfly and was located on the floor below. 'The good old days,' he sighed, when I got to talk to him a couple of years ago. When Hillbrow was still 'civilised', and the nightlife was still 'dazzling'. It was 'safe'. Barry knows how to make it clear, in carefully chosen terms, that things were so much better when there were no blacks living in Hillbrow.

It was a very disjointed conversation because every so often he would get up and go to the toilet, almost always with a detour, swiftly putting a little note in the hands of a black boy whom he fancied. That was his trademark. 'In the old days, the telephone didn't stop ringing: the next day, it was almost always bingo.' That tailed off too.

Not that he had a problem with the fact that, in the 1980s, blacks were allowed to visit Skyline. That actually came in quite handy, for now he did not have to go to the park any more, or the station. But because of the black influx, a lot of his white friends stopped coming to the pub and it became well nigh impossible 'to have a good conversation'. We should know that it is 'so much easier to take a black man out of the jungle than to take the jungle out of a black man'.

If there had been a pressure group called 'racists against apartheid', Barry would certainly have been a member. It is an intriguing irony: with his unstoppable desire to cross the colour bar he, like many others, actually contributed to the undermining of apartheid politics, but when that system finally went under, he himself became a victim of it.

So the story was that if you wanted a 'garden boy', you went to Skyline, or so Barry's friends, most of whom have now fled to Connections down the road, told him. But in the new South Africa the self-confidence of those who were once dependent on white patrons for a couple of rand or a place to stay is growing. The price then was simple: sex. Taken in the middle of the night, hidden in the boot, to the white suburbs. If you were caught the next morning in an area forbidden to blacks, it was assumed you would pretend to be the master's 'garden boy'. That was the way it was.

These days many of Skyline's black patrons live in Hillbrow or one of the surrounding areas, or have friends close by that they can rely on. Barry's comments express an intense longing for two things long lost to him: a more orderly time and system, and sex. I watch him now as he again accidentally falls against the young man on the bar stool next to him, who pushes him back in a friendly manner. Then he gets up and stumbles out of the bar.

Paul wrinkles his nose when I ask him whether Barry ever put a note in his hands. The minister, now almost thirty years old, of the gay church in Hillbrow was one of the first black patrons in Skyline. 'I had heard about the place from Simon, who was the very first, and one evening in 1985 I took the plunge. I was bloody nervous: after much hesitation, I made so bold as to go inside,' says Paul. 'The bar was still downstairs and it was full of whites. It was as if everybody was staring at me when I walked into the bar. Norman and Stephen, the barmen, said at first that it was actually not allowed but also that they had been told to ask patrons politely what they wanted to drink – and since I was a patron, they poured a Coke for me.'

According to Paul it is thanks to these decent family men from Soweto that the 'whites-only' policy was slowly eroded and was eventually officially scrapped by management.

'I think they saw the signs at an early stage and realised that if they wanted to keep this pub running, they'd better adapt,' says Stephen, who has worked for over twenty-five years in Butterfly/Skyline.

In the beginning it was not a comfortable place to be.

'Initially you did not go there for fun: it was more like making a statement,' says Paul. And, of course, sometimes one managed to break through the colour bar.

'Some whites were very friendly and confessed they had been looking forward to this for years.'

No, he'd never been a garden boy. 'But I was a newspaper boy.' Another excuse.

'Eventually,' he says, 'we felt welcome in Skyline. In Connections you were not even served a drink: there were white bartenders there.' And in the Dungeon, in town, the dancing was good but blacks were not allowed to go into the darkroom.

'Somebody would stroke your head and if he felt you had frizzy hair, you were pushed aside.' Apartheid in the darkroom.

▽▽▽

'The church is not doing at all well,' says Paul. 'Since our priest died, it's been going through a rough patch.' The charismatic priest had recently – and suddenly – died of complications from meningitis. He was dead within a week: the obituary spoke of a short illness. 'I think I'll drop out of it for a while. I don't know, but I don't think most people are honest.'

Shortly before the priest died, I had attended a church service.

'Why are we going to Skyline?' he asked rhetorically – and repeated the question at least five times, until one of the fifty or so churchgoers actually remembered the answer: 'To spread the word of God!'

Hallelujah!

The priest was visibly happy with such religious dedication.

I looked around and recognised some of the young men from other evenings at Skyline. They had danced, played billiards, courted each other, courted me. They were, in other words, very actively involved with this, that and quite a lot of the other. But spreading the word of the Lord? I had never actually noticed anybody doing so. Thabo, who is sitting in the front row in the hall in the hotel next to the bar, looks over his shoulder and winks at me.

'To go to Skyline', the priest is saying, 'is a blessed task.'

On a flip chart at the front of the church, he draws sketches of good and evil, to great public acclaim, of the holy trinity – all of this in a gay context. Meanwhile, the priest loses himself in reasoning that leads to the inevitable conclusion that He approves and that His Son might have been 'that way' too. And there is not a shadow of doubt among the audience as far as this is concerned. The hallelujahs follow one after the other.

Towards the end of the service, after many wonderfully rousing hymns, some of the churchgoers speak out. They testify of mothers who failed to understand them, of fathers addicted to drinking, of sisters who became victims of gang rape ... but in the end, everything turned out all right. Due to Him and His Word.

On the evening after a church service Thabo goes to Skyline. He is seventeen and has been living with the priest for some months. He is not the first to find a safe haven in the priest's flat, a place to find peace after his family had thrown him out.

'He is good to me,' he says, already a little bit tipsy on the brandy and Cokes which he has gulped down with impressive speed.

'It is just that I am not allowed to leave. He says that Skyline is the house of sin, and that only the seedy side of life goes there. Now he has gone to Durban for a conference, but if he finds out that I have been here tonight ...'

Thabo's entire body shivers.

'What is wrong with Skyline?' I ask. Wasn't it a 'blessed task' to go there?

'Everybody has got AIDS here.'

'How do you know?'

'He told me so.'

'And how does he know?'

'He counsels people.'

Then Thabo casts his eyes slowly about him, scanning the bar. Indicating several people around him, he says: 'That one has got AIDS, that one, and that one.'

'Have you heard about Heinrich?' Paul asks that same night. When I look questioningly at him, he says bluntly: 'Suicide.'

Paul puts a loving arm around Thabo's shoulder and makes it clear to him that it is time to go home. The young man can hardly stand up. Supported by Paul, he staggers towards the exit.

Heinrich, a middle-aged German immigrant, had been a regular at the pub for years. He was enormously popular and was always surrounded by young black men, who listened attentively to his many stories. Because we had some mutual friends, we always acknowledged each other but we had little to say to each other. Until one evening he sat himself down next to me and started talking to me: 'He iz so bjutiful. He iz gordjus! I sink I rielly love hiem.' He wanted to know whether Ayaz ever mentioned him. I had to disappoint him, shook my head and somehow failed to mention that my housemate actually hated him. Ayaz thought Heinrich was a creep, a Mr Fucking-Around-Number-One.

Heinrich ended our short conversation with: 'I thienk I wiel call hiem.'

Three days later a flower arrangement was delivered. The card read: 'I adore you.' Sender: Heinrich.

Ayaz was painfully taken by surprise with this gesture. After he had read the card, he went to the telephone and dialled the number of his German admirer. He thanked him for the flowers and asked Heinrich not to contact him ever again. When he had put the receiver down, he took the flowers to the kitchen, opened the window and threw them out. Not long after that, it became clear to me that Ayaz had managed to prevent himself from signing his own death warrant.

Several months later, Paul came to visit. 'Heinrich is HIV-positive and has known so for a number of years. But meanwhile he fucks around without a condom.' Paul swallowed a couple of times and continued, almost whispering: 'He has a list of names. I saw it myself. Two boys have died already. What am I to do?'

Despair was written all over Paul's face.

'Did you and he …?'

Paul was silent.

'We must turn him in to the police,' I suggested.

Paul was shocked and said determinedly: 'That is impossible.'

'Why not? He's a murderer.'

'Most of the boys are still in the closet. They are dead scared their families will find out.'

For an hour or so we sat opposite each other, feeling powerless.

'He thinks he's been infected by a black guy. He is just taking revenge,' Paul concluded. 'But perhaps I can help out.'

Within a few weeks it struck me that people no longer talked to Heinrich anymore. In the beginning, he still looked full of hope, waved at old friends, but they did not react. The news had spread via a carefully orchestrated rumour campaign. Those who might have been susceptible to his advances knew they were being watched by those who were determined to isolate the spreader of the virus. I could feel the aggression whenever the man entered the bar, a well-controlled reminder that this silent revenge showed no mercy whatsoever. After a month, he no longer showed up. In a certain sense it was an ominous sign. Could he now be going to look for his victims in parks and public toilets? There was a sigh of relief in the bar when Paul announced one evening that Heinrich had returned to Germany. He had heard this from his neighbour.

The rejoicing was, however, short-lived, for Heinrich returned shortly afterwards. Germany was cold, his homesickness unbearable, he had told Paul over the phone. Paul had turned down an invitation to drop by one of these days.

'His domestic worker found him in his bath. He had cut his wrists.' Paul has just dropped Thabo off at a taxi rank and sits down next to me again. 'Lonely, abandoned,' says Paul, somewhat shocked by the success of his own campaign.

I feel no remorse at all.

'He was buried this morning. His sisters came from Germany.'

How does he know?

'I was there. Along with Yusuf, Ketso, Sipho, Jabu ... everybody.'

Jesus. A serial killer buried in the presence of his possible future victims. An intriguing idea for a novel.

※※※

There are only a few whites that still go to Skyline and they are largely immigrants, recognisable by their Japanese, Eastern European, Greek, Italian or German accents.

And there is even what could be termed a Dutch 'community', a group of middle-aged men who have lived in the country for years. It was not so much apartheid politics that drew them here, but rather a sense of adventure, a longing for space, the spirit of enterprise. Over the years, I have come to realise that a simple condemnation of their politically incorrect choice is really only half the story. In many cases, a hidden motive was the most important reason for their choice.

There is the case of Bert, for instance, an estate agent who was expelled from a seminary in Brabant in the 1950s because of his sexual orientation. Ironically enough, he found sexual freedom in southern Africa, the home of apartheid and homophobic laws, a freedom that was at the time sorely lacking in the southern Netherlands. Cut off from his family and creatively navigating the colour bar, Bert had had the time of his life.

Now this group mixes with a new generation of Dutchmen, those who came to South Africa after 1990. Embarrassed and with my stomach churning, I regularly listen to the old guard's stories, torn between an understanding of their situation and an aversion to a barely respectful – at least at first sight – attitude towards black South Africa. Sometimes it appears as if they feel they are part of some kind of meat rack at Skyline. When someone shows some interest in any of the patrons, he is likely to be told: 'Oh, but I've had that one already.'

Over the years homesickness for Holland has increased, a phenomenon that seems to be becoming more common in immigrant communities. It is a desire for a Holland that no longer exists. They listen to old records by Wim Sonneveld in each other's homes and read books by Albert Mol, both gay artists famous in Holland in the sixties. Like many of their compatriots, they considered emigrating on the eve of Mandela's inauguration, but the privilege of their white existence outweighed their fear of change.

One such was Ronnie, a Dutch baker, a man whose speech was always peppered with clichés. Whenever anyone asked how he was, he always answered that 'a bad person can only do well'. He came to Johannesburg in the early 1960s. He got married and had children, but after his divorce he discovered gay life and took to it like a duck to water. There were always black boys around in his mansion. He picked them up in Skyline or from along the road. A fellow journalist once pointed out to me the places where these rent boys used to hang out. They cost him 'next to nothing'. His carefree behaviour eventually led to his downfall. When he invited me and my colleague over one Easter Sunday for a braai, we waited for hours in front of a closed gate with the other guests. There was no car; the front door was open. Eventually we decided to raise the alarm with the police. My colleague jumped over the gate with two policemen and went inside. A minute later he re-appeared in the doorway. 'He has been murdered. He has been murdered,' he shouted.

Ronnie was found tied to his bed, his throat pierced with a screwdriver.

The next few hours were bizarre. One of the guests ran inside and called Ronnie's ex-wife. He got her answering machine and yelled: 'Christine, you have to come at once. Ronnie has been murdered.' A little while later, a car pulled up in front of the house. A Dutchman jumped out and he, having been told the news, started to make telephone calls. He only seemed to be interested in Ronnie's business affairs. After a couple of hours, Jonas appeared on the scene. There were questions. That lanky young black man down there, wasn't he Ronnie's lover? Should he not be informed? After a while, the man who had telephoned Christine earlier, snapped at him and cold-bloodedly told him what had happened. Bluntly and making no bones about it. The traumatised young man asked whether he could collect some clothes from the house. He was not allowed to.

A tip-off from a man who had seen Ronnie's car in Hillbrow soon led to the arrest of two of the three men responsible. One of them had been a friend of Ronnie's in the past; he had let two men in that Saturday evening, apparently totally unsuspecting. What happened next is still difficult to work out. One of the suspects is still on the loose; the other two constantly contradicted each other during the trial. Ronnie's friend was released on a technicality. The presumed murderer was convicted to forty years in prison. My colleague, who was called to testify during the trial, felt torn between satisfaction and pity. It was a remark by Ronnie's gardener, who lived in, that kept on echoing in my colleague's head. He kept saying his employer was 'a man with a big heart'.

☙☙☙

The jukebox is on full blast. At the pool table a young man sings along, wildly gesticulating to Frank Sinatra's 'New York, New York'. A white woman in her seventies on the modest stage behind the bar attracts everyone's attention. She regularly accompanies her gay son to this bar. She pulls up her dress way above her knees and waves her left leg about, then the right leg. 'I want to fuck a black man, New York, New York,' the mother yells. Granny is quite literally carried away by the crowd after her Skyline preformance.

'At last, a queen mother,' says Simon Nkoli. After a long hiatus, he is finally going out again; thanks to the cocktail treatment that he has been taking of late, he has become stronger. He has more energy and he has also gained some weight. 'It would of course be better if we could find a black female patron,' says Nkoli. 'And we had hoped for Winnie, of course.'

During his prison years Nkoli was supported by the erstwhile 'mother of the nation'. She had visited him several times. It was one of her lawyers, George Bizos, already renowned for his defence of Mandela in the 1960s, who had given Nkoli's fellow prisoners a choice – accept his sexual preference or choose a different lawyer. However, Winnie greatly disappointed the gay movement in 1991. In what seemed an attempt to cover up her alleged involvement in the murder of fourteen-year-old township activist Stompie Seipei, all guilt was shifted onto a white Methodist priest. He was accused of having sexually abused members of Winnie's football team, among whom was Stompie. The kidnapping of the boys from his home to that of Winnie's was a 'rescue attempt'. It was not true – it was no more than a transparent attempt to gain the support of the black population by playing on homophobic sentiments. Without success, for that matter. Winnie has also lost her position as candidate queen mother for Nkoli, although, like many South Africans, he still feels sympathy for Nelson's ex-wife. 'I can understand her madness so well,' he says.

'Fortunately we still had Ma Thoko,' says Nkoli, 'but she's no longer alive.'

❦❦❦

There were, at the beginning of the 1990s, at least five gay shebeens in kwaThema, a township south of Johannesburg. And the first one was Ma Thoko's. The fifty-year-old woman found out in the course of the 1980s that her nephew was 'different'. She decided to open up her front room as a shebeen for his friends who were also 'like that'. They could not go anywhere else.

When I visited the shebeen in 1991, it was packed. From a ghetto blaster Michael Jackson's rousing music could be heard, the masses dancing under thick smoke clouds. The table was full of litre bottles of beer. Ma Thoko spoke to me in the tiny kitchen. She looked away most of the time. She has a simple explanation for the proverbial tolerance in this township. 'People don't find gays strange. Due to all the suffering in the past, there is something wrong with everybody.' Then she pointed out the little boy in the courtyard. 'That's Thami. Do you see how he moves? I already know he is gay.'

In a corner of the pub sat two young men holding hands. Their names were British and Irish. They took me on a pub crawl that night. Theirs is a depressing story. Some months after I met them British died of the wounds inflicted on him by his brother. His brother did not approve of all that 'stuff with men' and in a drunken frenzy British was assaulted with a pitchfork. He was in bed for weeks and there was no money for hospital treatment. When the GLOW activists finally took him to the hospital in nearby Springs, it was already too late. Shortly after British's death, I visited his mother together with one of the original GLOW activists. What was there to say? Everything except for the truth. British had had an accident while playing tennis, that's how it happened, she said. Later, in the hospital, medical registrar Greyling was put out when we asked him why he had not informed the police. 'Do you realise that the only thing we do here is sew people up?'

But wasn't this attempted manslaughter or murder? 'Sir, there is such a big cultural gap between what we consider just and what they consider just' was the response.

About a hundred GLOW members attended British's funeral. When the priest observed that the reason for his death was his dealing with 'strange people', they called out: 'We are these strange people!' And Simon Nkoli referred to British in a short speech as 'a gay Steve Biko'.

'I think I'm spending half of my time at funerals,' sighs Nkoli, putting his arm around Irish. British's lover has meanwhile found a new partner, with whom he has just entered the bar. 'It's two years since Ma Thoko died. A consequence of her diabetes,' he says. 'Her shebeen is closed, but others have taken its place: kwaThema stays gay,' he says with a smile.

▿▿▿

The evening passes very quickly. Shortly before two, Norman and Stephen call for last orders. People get ready to leave, to go home or to go on to Club 58, a pub just down the road where all of Africa is drawn together and some patrons boast about the number of nationalities they have so far scored there.

Back at Skyline, the jukebox is switched off, the neon lights are put on and the almost deserted pub suddenly resembles a somewhat neglected waiting room at a train station.

As I'm getting ready to leave and stand up, a young man in a red jersey comes hesitatingly towards me.

'Are you ...?'

Then I recognize him: Linda's nephew.

We walk to the exit. 'It's already five years ago that we buried him,' says Learnmore. I remember a baking hot church in Soweto, packed with members of Linda's confessional church and GLOW activists. I remember Linda himself, one of the founding members of the gay movement, who had shown me round in the township shortly after the first Pink Saturday. 'My father has stopped being difficult about it,' he had told me, 'as long as I don't sleep with members of the congregation.'

But when the young man suddenly passed away the father opened his heart at a GLOW memorial service. He had indeed found peace with Linda's homosexuality, but those dresses, was that really necessary? It was confusing for the ancestors. What would they think on looking into the houses of their black descendants in Soweto and finding a house full of Indians? What would they think if they looked into his house and saw his son in female guise? That was not possible, was it?

Some GLOW members had a good laugh about this; others became very angry. Their revenge was sweet. During the funeral service and before hundreds of white-clad deeply religious women two boys in dresses had seated themselves next to Linda's coffin and stood guard for hours on end.

We recall this while walking outside. 'I went to Skyline tonight out of respect for Linda. I have never been here before. I'm not gay,' Learnmore confesses. 'I understand where his father was coming from. I also found those dresses weird. I was crazy about him but that I didn't understand.'

Skyline is an eye-opener. 'Now it's easier to understand. All those different people. Nobody is aggressive. I'm pretty sure Linda was very happy here.'

Mangosuthu Dlamini did not beat around the bush. In March 1997, in a press release sent out to all Swazi newspapers, he announced the establishment of a gay movement in the kingdom of Swaziland: GALESWA, the Gays and Lesbians of Swaziland. He was prepared to give interviews, it was announced – a courageous provocation in a country that cherished its Victorian anti-gay laws and enforced these with more fanaticism than anywhere else in the region.

The media responded eagerly to Dlamini's offer. The interviews were illustrated with a photograph of a twenty-one-year-old man. He posed in a neat striped suit with a broad smile and with both his index fingers pointing forward. But where had I seen this face before?

He told a simple story: 'We live on the threshold of the twenty-first century. Neighbouring South Africa protects its citizens against discrimination on the grounds of sexual orientation. Swaziland must stop pretending gays do not exist.' Dlamini knew better. In the first few weeks after the establishment of GALESWA, the group gained over eighty members, among whom were 'children still in primary school'.

For weeks on end, Dlamini's provocative story dominated the editorial pages of the newspapers. This gave rise to a debate among heterosexuals. The Prime Minister, also a Dlamini, stated that the government would 'continue considering homosexuals as abnormal until the Swazi community accepts this minority'.

Chairperson Mayisela of the Medical Institute of Southern Africa said he had no problems with gays at all. 'I respect the right of anyone to a preference of their own.'

Doctor Ntiwane blamed homosexual behaviour on 'bad influences' and an 'urge to experiment among youngsters. Conventional medicine does not give a definite answer on whether homosexuality is natural or not.'

Father Magongo, a Catholic priest, encouraged the nation not to discriminate but to show understanding and pray a lot.

In the *Times of Swaziland*, the editors went for each other's throats. Under the heading 'Down with gays!' the columnist Vusie Ginindza referred to homosexuality as 'social syphilis'. Society should be protected against these 'termites'. 'If sodomy is created by God, please send me to hell' was Ginindza's conclusion.

The chief editor of the Sunday edition of the newspaper, Bheki Makhubu, responded to him in an equally passionate contribution. 'If there is a group of people in this country that deserve to be held in contempt, it is the priesthood. They sleep around with married women, are guilty of raping children, are silent about the fact that almost every week there is somebody on trial who has abused a two-year-old baby and then they advise the king to murder homosexuals … Why does no one say anything when murderers are not prosecuted because they are connected to the royal family? And if the Bible is the measuring stick for human behaviour, why does nobody condemn polygamy?'

The public debate inspired the *Times* to an April Fool's Day prank. 'Wonders will never cease. Take that accursed gay chief Mangosuthu Dlamini, for instance. He has managed to reveal the hypocrisy of his attackers.' The newspaper claimed to be in possession of videotapes showing prominent Swazis committing 'sodomy'. In a scene shot in a house in Manzini, Mangosuthu allegedly makes love to a 'prominent church leader'; in another scene, a top-ranking government official allegedly indulges himself in 'gentlemen's love'. The article ended with: 'The video is available from all local bookstores.'

❦❦❦

'Pest,' Nigel Forbes mumbles, taking a sip of his scotch. The eighty-year-old Brit has lived his whole life in Swaziland, living off the capital that his grandfather earned from gold prospecting. By the autumn of 1998, the controversy sparked by Mangosuthu Dlamini has faded but Forbes can still get angry about it. He sees the attempt to establish a gay movement as a mere fad, a whim of fashion, as outrageous as the 'communist trade unions' and the human rights organisations that plead for a lifting of the state of emergency and the introduction of a multi-party system – he utters each phrase with ill-disguised disgust.

The Swazi are not interested in this sort of thing at all, he thinks, ignoring the success of recent strikes and the joining of forces of opposition groups. On the veranda of his wooden bungalow, just outside the capital Mbabane, the old man muses endlessly on 'the' Swazi and 'his' history.

His gaze carefully follows the two young gardeners who attend to the lawn. 'Nice pieces,' he says, drying his whisky-wet lips with a white handkerchief. 'But what do they know of democracy? That belongs to the West. Swaziland is a traditional kingdom where the Dlaminis call the shots.'

As a consequence of royal polygamy, almost half a million Swazis are called Dlamini.

'Mswati III, the present king, chooses a new bride every year during the reed ceremony, on the eve of the harvesting season.

Then thousands of virgins, who are not Dlaminis, come together in the open field, bare-breasted.'

The nervous twitch at the left corner of Forbes's mouth, and his impressive eyebrows that rise up and down, appear to show a slight distaste for all this; but that impression is rejected indignantly.

'No, that is the way it should be. Other families become related by marriage to the Dlaminis in this way, and they simultaneously safeguard their authority in this way. All power to the king and his chiefs. We're in Africa here.'

A proliferation of African curios and prints in the bungalow points to a certain nostalgia for the past that he shares with the traditionalists in Swaziland. He is a romantic who sees any change as a threat.

'Look, this is Mswati I. He built up the kingdom from 1840. He was dead scared of the Zulus. After the umpteenth attack, he was given an audience by Sir Theophilus Shepstone in Natal. In order to please him, Mswati offered him one of his sisters. Shepstone declined in a friendly manner, but promised to support all Swazis against those damned Zulus,' Forbes says as we walk past the prints in the passage.

'His successor was called Ludongo, a very attractive man. He sold almost all of Swaziland. The Europeans were given concessions to work the land, to dig for gold, to regulate public transport, to build hotels. Even the import of spirits, of peppermint, the running of a lottery and the issuing of money were privatised. Those were the days.'

At the portrait of King Mbandeni, who succeeded Ludongo when the newly arrived white adventurers had meanwhile set up a form of home rule, Forbes says:

'Under him the boundaries were drawn. In 1880 he was invited for a consultation with the Portuguese governor of Mozambique, Von Wieligh of the Boer Republic of Transvaal and Colonel Martin, the commander of Natal. When he woke up in the morning, his servants brought him traditional beer. Thereupon the Portuguese governor offered him a whisky. Thereafter Martin poured him a glass of gin and Von Wieligh a glass of champagne. Heavily intoxicated, Mbandeni signed an agreement which cost him a considerable amount of his land. Back in Swaziland he forbade his family ever to touch alcohol.' Forbes' story degenerates into thunderous laughter.

When evening falls, a heavy drizzle and a thick blanket of cloud slowly descend over the hills that surround the city. The boys in the garden have meanwhile put on their jeans and thank the master for the five emalangeni (six rand) that he slips into their hands. They walk hand in hand to the end of the grounds, watched by Forbes until they disappear from sight. Then he turns to me and says: 'I have been fascinated all my life by the physical beauty of the Swazi. It has got nothing to do with sex. That never interested me – it spoils everything.'

When we say goodbye, Forbes again bemoans the 'foreign influences' that threaten to overwhelm the Swazi cultural heritage. But there is light at the end of the tunnel.

'One of the tribal chiefs has pressed for the appointment of a hangman. The previous one, a South African, left eight years ago. Judges hand down death penalties, but there is nobody to do the dirty work.'

Meanwhile, an advertisement has appeared in the newspapers. Women are also allowed to apply.

'Whatever happened to Mangosuthu Dlamini?' I ask him on the way out. 'Never heard of him again,' Forbes says tersely. 'That picture has been printed over twenty times in the newspaper. A native in a striped suit, who seems to indicate the length of his male member with his pointed index fingers. Disgusting.'

The next day, in a coffee shop in the centre of town, I try

Dlamini's telephone number – the one printed in the newspaper the previous year. Next to the telephone is a round table – girls of about sixteen sit at it drinking beer.

Nobody answers the phone.

❦❦❦

It is perhaps a little tragic that the People's United Democratic Movement (PUDEMO) starts its desperate written pleas for international support with the sentence 'Where is Swaziland?' Even people with some geographical knowledge tend to think the country is a province of South Africa.

Mario Masuku giggles constantly when I tell him of my meeting with Forbes. But his cheerfulness, evident from his reaction to the picture he has of this aged colonial relic, is in marked contrast to the bitter tone of his exposé on the post-colonial authorities.

'In 1990 we organised a congress and decided to establish PUDEMO. We demanded abolition of the state of emergency, which had been announced in 1973, five years after independence. We advocated a multi-party system, a free trade union and a free press. Immediately after the congress, I was arrested together with nine others. I spent many months in detention.'

According to Masuku, the attraction traditionalists have for the Swazi cultural heritage serves no other purpose than to keep the power of the chiefs and tribal elders in place: a feudal system that many Swazis have had enough of.

The PUDEMO chairperson reacted eagerly to my request for a meeting. There are only a few foreign journalists that show any interest in the developments in his country. He pushes a number of requests for financial support into my hand, hoping that these will find their way to a Dutch development organisation via me.

But is there no support from the ANC? Exiled members of the organisation enjoyed years of hospitality in safe houses in the kingdom, didn't they? This appears to be a painful question, which Masuku will only address more openly later in the conversation. I sense much bitterness in his observation that Mandela's movement avoids any engagement in Swaziland for exactly the same reason that the erstwhile apartheid regime used to prevent Western countries from supporting the ANC: one should not interfere in 'internal affairs'.

▽▽▽

On the way to neighbouring Manzini, the National Museum of Swaziland draws my attention. A friendly guide leads me to a kraal and explains to me a local custom. Thus I learn that it was customary to marry girls during a raid. 'When it is dark, a young man would secretively enter the hut of a young girl. If he was not intercepted, she would have to make love to him. Once she has slept with him, she must marry him,' the guide explains. A deputy director of the South African prison services called this custom 'interesting', according to a note in the visitors' book. But I understand better now why girls of sixteen spend their lunchtime sipping beer.

At last the telephone is answered. But the woman on the other end of the line just says 'No, no' when I ask for Mangosuthu Dlamini. 'Of GALESWA,' I try again cautiously, but she does not respond.

By sheer coincidence I am close to wrapping up this story when I call at a petrol station in Manzini. A beautiful young black man with bleached hair comes walking out of the store and, if I'm not mistaken, he's 'family'. I smile at him in a friendly manner and he returns my smile. Then I take a gamble and say: 'GALESWA?'

Bingo! He shakes my hand and says that his name is Sibusiso and yes, he was a member. But the organisation is pretty well dead. 'On account of Mangosuthu,' he says. 'He is in prison.'

A strange feeling comes over me, a combination of journalistic excitement and shock. Does Mangosuthu Dlamini pay for his heroism with incarceration?

No. 'He's a thief,' says Sibusiso with a snigger. 'Stole money at work. This doesn't do the cause any good.'

On my way back to South Africa, I suddenly remember why Dlamini's photo was so familiar. His face was on a notice on a wall at Skyline. 'Wanted,' it read, 'because he stole my cellphone.' And all of a sudden I recall that note in the minutes of the Rainbow Project in Windhoek. 'The benefit was a great success. A couple of thousands of dollars have been collected.' It was just a great pity that that 'young man from Swaziland', who had so enthusiastically given his all to the organisation, had run away with the cash register.

Pest.

It is as if somebody has switched on a light in the southern African twilight. Perhaps that is a pity for the herd boy in northern Namibia or the mineworker in the Botswana hostel who enjoy their flings under the cover of darkness without having to construct an identity for themselves or be part of a subculture. A twilight zone does have its advantages. Homo, hetero, bi ... these seem to be suffocating straitjackets, excluding so much more than they allow.

But it is a highly visible step forward. The fact that young gays and lesbians in the southern part of Africa now dare to go public is undoubtedly positive. The piles of letters in the offices of organisations in Johannesburg, Harare and Windhoek attest to this. Requests for information and appeals for help no longer fall on deaf ears. The possibility of identification means people no longer feel isolated. Quite a number of people feel encouraged to take steps they did not consider possible before. Others feel threatened by the new openness. Appealing to culture and tradition, they seek to stop the inevitable. But the deeper I went into the southern part of Africa over those final few months, the more convinced I became that things are not much different from the situation in my own country, Holland. Shortly before I completed this book, a Dutch friend of mine told me about the documentary she was preparing for television. It was about an old-age home for gays in the Jordaan area of Amsterdam. Her focus was on two residents, both of whom had lived their whole lives in the predominantly working-class area. And they find it very difficult, even in Holland, to speak openly. When my friend said to one of them, 'Why don't you just say "I am gay?"' the reaction was: 'Are you crazy?'

Even in the Jordaan homosexuality dare not speak its name.

The year 1999 is almost over. Nearly two years have passed since I ended my investigations throughout the southern African region and the time has come for me to record and conclude the findings of my journey.

Much water has passed under the moffie bridge since then. In Botswana, a modest gay movement called Legabibo has been established. A similar attempt in Zambia failed when it became obvious that a local human rights organisation saw an opportunity in the initiative to strengthen its own profile. The human rights group saw a chance to obtain foreign funding: the gay activists never saw a cent of it. It is a phenomenon that is unfortunately not unknown elsewhere in the region. The Zambian gay activists have meanwhile disbanded and operate more or less underground after a national radio broadcaster publicised the establishment of the Alliance Against People With Abnormal Sexual Behaviour, a vigilante group.

Verbal attacks by Presidents Museveni (Uganda) and Arap Moi (Kenya) have temporarily created a strong homophobic wind across the African continent in the African spring of 1999. This certainly put a damper on the mood of the representatives from the eleven African countries who united at the conference of the International Lesbian and Gay Association in Johannesburg in September 1999. One positive outcome is that the media in the different countries, other than in Zimbabwe, used the attacks as springboards for debate rather than sycophantically supporting them.

The doyen of East African intellectuals, Professor Ali Mazrui, has in the meantime tried to come to the rescue of the burgeoning gay movement. 'Governments such as those in Zimbabwe and Uganda seem to be more concerned about homosexuality than corruption,' he said in early October.

Meanwhile in South Africa, the homophobic statutes continue to be erased from the penal code after the adoption of the new constitution in 1996, guaranteeing freedom of sexual orientation. An ANC conference has also declared itself in favour of gay marriage, but it is likely that quite a few delegates were guided by considerations of morality rather than a genuine concern for lesbian and gay equality. Many people probably consider married gays to be more decent than unmarried ones. And that's not really so different from European views on the subject ...

The feared religious fundamentalist reaction to the South African winds of change has not really got off the ground, in spite of attempts by the Cape Town–based People Against Gangsterism and Drugs (PAGAD) or the African Christian Democratic Party (ACDP) to kindle that particular homophobic fire. However, in mid-November 1999 a gay bar in Cape Town was the target of a bomb attack in which six people were injured. The incident is perhaps a reminder that one should be careful not to lose sight of reality. PAGAD appears to have lost a large section of its support while the ACDP has only a handful of representatives in Parliament; but both groups link up perfectly in their agitation around still broadly popular prejudices that exist across a wide spectrum of communities. It may now be politically correct to hold a tolerant point of view about homosexuality, but what do people really think deep down?

❧❧❧

When, in the spring of 1998, the leader of the National Party, Marthinus van Schalkwyk, was accused of having oral sex with a coloured gardener, he responded with an outspoken denial.

Van Schalkwyk said he could not be gay because he was a 'boereseuntjie'. When the derisive laughter which this statement caused in the gay bars of Pretoria penetrated into the offices of the party leadership, the NP leader went out of his way to state that he had not intended to insult gays. But he had done so, and he no doubt had the approval of a lot of people who are utterly fed up with all those talk shows on radio and television where the gay and lesbian movement pleads its cause, let alone all those films with a gay theme on the SABC.

How difficult it is to give up entrenched ideas became clear during the conference of the World Council of Churches in Harare in December 1998. In spite of all lobbying activities, GALZ could barely get a foot in the door in order to express its views. The chairperson of the South African Human Rights Commission, Dr Barney Pityana, refused requests to fly the flag for the gay movement in his address to the congress on rather formal grounds – he had already submitted his speech to the organisers. This disappointed quite a number of people. However, he redeemed himself in July 1999 with an address to the Institute for Contextual Theology in Johannesburg, the content of which was almost sacrilegious for a theologian. Pityana stated, for instance, that he had difficulty with the Bible, as with all publications that are given eternal value. To condemn homosexuality on the basis of dated texts was, consequently, something he rejected. The tendency of Christians 'to know everything' and to 'play God' filled him with dismay. Pityana referred to the gay movement as 'one of the most influential interest groups' and said he was 'proud to be associated with the struggle of gays and lesbians for the freedom of sexual orientation'. In the discussion that followed, Pityana strongly dismissed the reproach that 'the South African constitution is, in fact, un-African'. He stated: 'If that is true, then African culture is inherently unjust.'

What is African or un-African? A Mozambican friend whose family looks down on him because he is homosexual, every so often sends money to Maputo. Perhaps this will help his family accept his sexual preference. He thinks that I find his behaviour strange, but his way of behaving is 'African': 'That is the way we do things over here.' Indeed I find his behaviour strange, but that it is 'African' seems to me to be sheer nonsense. In the slums of New Delhi, or in rural Albania, poor people show as much flexibility when a change in their system of norms and values results in financial gain.

That the Zimbabwean ex-President Canaan Banana – found guilty of sexually abusing his former bodyguard – now follows in the footsteps of his successor by also condemning homosexuality as 'un-African' seems to me to be an expression of the cowardly capacity for self-denial for which so many missionaries before him had the blueprint.

That quite a number of white gays, especially in South Africa, now tend to come out of the closet as homosexuals but stay inside as whites is grist to the mill of black compatriots who, in the name of tradition and culture, condemn the preference as a 'Western import'. *The Gay Pages 1999*, a publication that attempts to capitalise on the 'pink rand', contains a revealing editorial in this regard. According to chief editor Van Niekerk, research has shown that the 'gay community primarily consists of the higher income groups'.

That might be true for the clientele of gay establishments in Rosebank, previously an exclusively white suburb, but not for those in kwaThema, still very much a black township.

The South African gay movement owes its success in the first place to the realisation by its founding mothers and fathers – Simon Nkoli, Beverley Ditsie, Donné Rundle, Edwin Cameron, Zackie Achmat, Sheila Lapinsky, Paul Mokheti and others – that the struggle for equal treatment could not be separated from the struggle against apartheid and poverty. The aforementioned banner of the Gays and Lesbians of the Witwatersrand (GLOW) that stood proudly at the memorial service for the assassinated ANC leader Chris Hani spoke volumes in that regard. Their struggle, our struggle.

Due to this association with the democratic movement, respect for and eventual approval of gay orientations was inevitable. Peter Vale, a South African academic, praised the Zimbabwean gay movement a couple of years ago for the fact that it was the first to dare to contradict the authorities in that country. Now that this has become widely accepted, GALZ might let the lesson from South Africa sink in. It is encouraging that trade union leader Morgan Tsvangirai, who is playing a central role in the creation of a democratic alternative, has since declared himself against shop-floor discrimination on the grounds of sexual preference, but what can GALZ's grass-roots support in its turn contribute to the reinforcement of Tsvangirai's struggle?

What can the leaders of the Namibian Rainbow Project, who have since joined Ben Ulenga's Congress of Democrats, contribute to the success of this broad coalition which has dragged the antediluvian SWAPO into the twenty-first century?

And conversely, how can Van Niekerk and his supporters use the power of the pink rand to support the historically disadvantaged, that is, black gays and lesbians?

As I write these final sentences for the English edition, the face of Simon Nkoli stares at me. The picture, dug out from a box on the day of his death, 30 November 1998, and taken a couple of years before by Kadir van Lohuizen, hangs on the wall of my office. That's him – a proud man who, as in all pictures of him, seems bigger than he was in reality; a gentle, caring gaze; a T-shirt announcing his homosexuality; a portrait of Mandela in the background. Even when I leave my flat for a while I am reminded of him. We lived in the same building during his last years. The door of his flat on the other side of the gallery, which was always open, is now closed.

Memories. A meeting of sixty representatives from Johannesburg to the Gay Games in Amsterdam, a full house. The dinner party in honour of the gay South African guests at the residence of Ambassador Carl Niehaus in The Hague. The final of the African Cup of Nations, won by Bafana Bafana (after which Simon dressed up in a female MK guerrilla outfit and disappeared into the festive crowd).

Then that Sunday morning.

'Please come,' asks Peter, who took care of him during his last weeks. 'He's ...'

'Dying?'

Then eyes from which the life has almost drained, a hand that appears to feel my touch, mumbling from which Peter, after trying to understand for a long time, makes out that he wants some water. When his mother comes, we make space.

Roderick, his lover, stands in the doorway.

'How are you?' I ask.

'Fine.' Politeness on autopilot. We're not fine at all.

When the male nurses carry the stretcher out of the house, I put bread and juice in the kitchen. Life goes on.

One day later Paul phones. Simon is dead. Shortly after three, Simon's light was extinguished. His death has meanwhile given the city council of Johannesburg cause to officially proclaim the street corner next to Skyline in Hillbrow Simon Nkoli Corner. And the annual conference of the International Lesbian and Gay Association, which took place in Johannesburg in September 1999 – for the first time in Africa and with representatives from more than ten African countries – turned into an impressive homage to one of the people who had switched on a light in this dark continent.

Synonyms for gay and lesbian descriptors

after nines – black gays who pretend to be heterosexuals at work and who reveal their true colours in the evening

agtermekaarkêrels – homosexual (Afrikaans)

bukhontxana – marriage between two mineworkers; literally: fucking between the thighs (Zulu)

drag or *drag queen* – male transvestite

dyke – lesbian (English)

family/familie – homosexual

fopdosser – transvestite (Afrikaans)

golda – Jewish gay (gay slang originating among Cape coloureds)

injonga – literally: young man who fucks

iris – Indian homosexual (gay slang originating among Cape coloureds)

kgwete – very recent term for homosexual; literally: somebody who is powerful, beautiful and unique (Tswana, Sesotho)

koffiemoffie – term for coloured homosexual, or for an air steward employed by South African Airways (SAA)

lettie – a lesbian (gay slang originating among Cape coloureds)

mapoto – the passive one, the 'wife' in a miners' marriage (Shona)

matonyola – literally: they who stick their penis into a man (Tswana, Sesotho)

mavis – a homosexual (slang originating among Cape coloureds)

moffie – Afrikaans for poof or fag. Slang and often derogatory word for homosexuals, usually male. The term 'moffie' is first mentioned in South African sea slang from 1929. A 'mophy' is a derogatory term among seafarers for delicate, well-groomed young men. Difference of opinion on the origin of the word. Possibly a bastardisation of 'mofrodite' (castrated Italian opera singer), or derived from the Dutch word 'mof' (article of clothing) or, less probable, the English word 'mauve' (a colour associated by some with homosexuality).

natalie – a black homosexual (gay slang originating among Cape coloureds)

ngotshana – marriage between two mineworkers, generally a term indicating homosexuality (Shona)

pantsula – macho young man who picks up transvestites or feminine young men (Zulu)

skesane – literally: young man who wants to be fucked (Zulu)

stabane/setabane – literally: somebody with two sexes, commonly a term of abuse for homosexuals (Zulu)

wendy – white homosexual (gay slang originating among Cape coloureds)

Gay and lesbian organisations in southern Africa

Botswana
Lesbians, Gays and Bisexuals of Botswana (Legabibo),
e-mail: acenter@ino.bw

Namibia
The Rainbow Project (TRP), P.O. Box 26122, Windhoek,
fax (061) 23 6371, e-mail: trp@iafrica.com

South Africa
National Coalition for Gay and Lesbian Equality (NCGLE),
36 Grafton Road, Yeoville, Johannesburg,
telephone (011) 487 2964, e-mail: evert@ncgle.org.za
Gay and Lesbian Archives of South Africa (GALA),
telephone (011) 716 2818, e-mail: galasa@pixie.co.za

Zimbabwe
Gays and Lesbians of Zimbabwe (GALZ), 35 Colenbrander Avenue, Milton Park, Harare, P.O. Box A6131, Avondale, Harare, telephone (034) 741 736, e-mail: galz@samara.co.zw

Website on gay and lesbian affairs
Behind The Mask: http://www.mask.org.za